UNCENSORED. UNTAMED. UNLEASHED.

HOW SOULFUL ENTREPRENEURS ARE LEADING INTO THE GOLDEN AGE

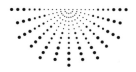

PUBLISHING

CONTENTS

INTRODUCTION

I was on a Zoom call with a friend and client when these words rolled off my tongue...

If you can see through it, you are meant to lead through it.

We are living in a time of great illusion and fear — but the good news is — there are so many whose eyes are wide open.

This book was born out of a desire to raise the vibration of the planet, so even more can begin to awake to not only what is true — but who they were born to be.

We must move beyond conflict and separation, into perfect and unconditional love. As one of my teachers says, "We must become what they wish to destroy."

What if each of us remembered who we really are, and what our gift to this world is?

What would it look like if we woke up asking how we could be a blessing today?

Being a leader has nothing to do with power or control, but everything to do with going first. It is time to model what we believe and teach.

And remember, when it feels like it's all too much, the challenge is the path.

There is always a next step, and there is always a way through.

As you read these inspiring stories, know they are reflecting what's inside of you.

You are holding this book for a reason — I can't wait for you to discover why.

This is for the loud ones, those who will not dim their light, or deny their divinity!

Adriana Monique Alvarez

ADRIANA MONIQUE ALVAREZ

THERE IS NO NEW EARTH WITHOUT A NEW ME AND YOU

We have been plunged into the deep end. Like it or not.

We have seen things for what they are. We have seen people for who they are. It has been both necessary and nauseating.

While much of my life has not changed, I have felt the war that is waging.

I became the hermit, which is the exact opposite of who I have always been. I was born a social bug, talking non-stop and always looking for a new adventure.

I stayed home a lot this year. I took a million walks by the river. I unplugged and left social media. I colored and cooked. I watched the clouds float by, and I began to sync up with nature and the rhythm of life.

I began to see *we* are the new in the New Earth.

I accepted the invitation to tune in. What I found is that it no longer makes sense for society to continue to…

1. Worry about money.
2. Work without rest.
3. Live without play.

I went deep into each of these, and began to see how deeply ingrained they are in us as a society. I began asking people about these three, and most were very honest that they simply were unwilling to give them up.

They didn't know what to do with themselves if this wasn't their life.

I began to think about how these habits form our identity. For years, they influenced the persona I lead with. After living overseas as a volunteer in my 20's, I returned to the U.S. with malaria, and an overwhelming sense that my choices made zero sense to a society that values higher education and climbing the corporate ladder. I had done neither. Nor had I married money and started a family.

I had not "chosen wisely," according to popular opinion.

I could feel the pressure to figure out how to "live in the real world."

I wanted nothing more than to return to a life without internet, social media, the American Dream, and the non-stop message of consumption. The problem was I would soon turn 28, and I was becoming the straight A student who was a disappointment to everyone.

So I put on my big-girl pants and dedicated the last 14 years to mastering business. I checked off all the boxes, and while I feel grateful for what I have learned, the people I have met, and how my children have been provided for — I often found myself missing the volunteer I used to be.

I missed the luxury of:

1. Believing I am always provided for.
2. That effort does not equate abundance.
3. Simply enjoying life right now.

I knew this was showing up to remind me my number one priority was to live like these are true. I have not done it perfectly, and it has been pretty annoying for some that I am unwilling to keep my old persona, but it has been incredibly worth it.

One thing I often told myself this year was, "I cannot live in an old way and expect anything new."

It might not make sense to relax, to rest, and to play while a war is being waged, but a friend frequently reminds me that all we must do right now is embody what they seek to destroy.

We are in a great battle right now, even though no bombs are dropping overhead. But make no mistake about it — principalities and powers in high places are in a full-on war.

This isn't about flesh and blood and being at odds with anyone... This is a war for the souls of this planet. This is a war of consciousness. The God gene is at risk, but the good news is — light wins. Always.

We will witness everything that once was seen as unshakable, fall. And we will all be given the opportunity to participate in a completely new way of living and being.

You didn't choose to be here so you could sit in the back row and eat popcorn. You are here to actively participate in the Great Awakening.

Find your new position.

Get your new assignment.

Step into it fully.

This probably has nothing to do with what you have done for a living —and yet—your heart cannot deny it.

Pray.
Mobilize supernatural support.
Be in nature.
Draw on ancient wisdom.
Be mindful.
Give your body only the best.
Grow food.
Heal yourself.
Find your gift.
Tell your children what matters.
Use your voice.
Cook with love.
Tell your story.
Be with family.
Love deeply.

In 2018, we visited a museum in Naples, Italy. It was a cool rainy day, and as I stepped in a side room, the piece of art pulled me closer. It was an Amazonian woman on a horse in battle. Her face was determined, and her arrow was drawn.

I could not take my eyes off of it.

And then I heard the words that gave me chills down my body... "A day will come when you will be asked to be this woman."

A year later, I was sitting on my white leather couch in New Orleans when I heard the 2 week announcement. Derek was right next to me, and the boys were playing on the floor, but I was transported back to the painting and heard, "It's time!"

How do we experience something new? Simple — we create it! The old is falling and the new is up to us.

Creation requires us to give up the endless work and move into play. Creation is tapping into the most God-like part of us there is. Creation feels good, and it requires permission from no one. You were born knowing how to do it, and you are remembering!

I invite you to stop second-guessing yourself, your ideas, your timing, and your abilities.

We do not have any time to debate, "Why you?"

Why not you?

Follow the nudges and unleash yourself!

Go.

We need you.

Now.

You have what it takes.

You always have.

Thank you for being the *new* in the New Earth!

ABOUT THE AUTHOR

Imagine a world without gatekeepers and censorship. *This* is what inspired Adriana Monique Alvarez to start AMA Publishing, and train a global network of female-owned publishing houses. She's a USA Today bestselling author, and can be seen in *Forbes, Entrepreneur, Huffington Post, International Living, America Daily Post, London Daily Post,* and *Grit Daily.*

She is currently living in "the middle-of-nowhere" Colorado, where she is renovating her grandparents' home, and learning how to homestead with her husband, Derek, and two sons, Sam and Grant.

Website: *www.AdrianaMoniqueAlvarez.com*

2

BRIDGET AILEEN SICSKO

THE RECLAMATION - STOP OUTSOURCING YOUR TRUTH

Born, we are free, yet we live lives that don't resemble freedom.
Each waking moment, we submit our power to others, giving away the highest
connection to our own intuitive guidance.
When will we return to the true knowingness of who we are?
The time is now.

I believe we are born free, yet through a series of funny events called life, we move as far away from that freedom as possible.

From a very young age, we constantly outsource our truth by listening to "experts" that know us better than ourselves.

The constant noise of society—the news, TV, media, music, education system—can feel extremely loud.

How are we meant to think for ourselves when we are constantly being bombarded with views other than our own?

I am twenty-eight years old as I write this. In my early teens, I had a massive awakening after a Lyme disease diagnosis. Doctor after doctor after doctor. Antibiotic rounds galore. And still, I was struggling.

I will never forget the day—or really, days—leading up to a very special doctor's appointment. At this time in my healing journey, I began to realize that the body is all connected. All cells, tissues, bones, organ systems, blood flow... connected. So, I decided that I should bring a document of my entire medical history to the gastroenterologist who was preparing me for a colonoscopy. It took me hours to sort through all diagnoses, supplements, antibiotics and blood work findings. I put it all in a folder and brought it with me to my appointment. Toward the end of the appointment, I told him I had compiled my full medical history to make it easier for him to get to the root cause.

He didn't look at it.

I remember leaving that doctor's office, sobbing in the car with my mom.

"He didn't look, Mom; he didn't *even* look."

Although not glaringly obvious to my pre-teen self at the time, this experience planted the greatest seed in my entrepreneurial and leadership journey, only to be fully realized and recognized over ten years later.

After that emotionally charged encounter, I set out on a journey to learn as much as I could about holistic health, Ayurveda, nutrition, herbs, mindset, and lifestyle.

And something I realized along the way was that these modalities were rooted in bringing the power back to the individual.

For example, Ayurveda is known as the sister science of yoga and is a medical system focused on mind and body balance. One of the core principles is that illness and disease are simply indicators of an imbalance. The idea is that we are born whole, and then, through a series of events called life, we move away from that balanced center. We consume GMO and pesticide-laden foods that have sat on trucks for far too long, stay in toxic relationships that have no boundaries, sit hunched over at desks for hours per day, staring at screens and ultimately live lives completely disconnected from nature. Ayurveda teaches that each person is unique, and what might be medicine for one person might be poison to another. I fell in love with this system that honored *me* and my unique healing journey.

As I began to study more and dive deeper into personal development, spiritual and cosmic law, it dawned upon me that many of the systems this world is built upon take our power away, whether knowingly or unknowingly.

It's become pretty clear to me that I have this unwillingness to compromise myself, my values or my dreams. Since I was young, I gladly left sports teams, organizations, and jobs that didn't feel in alignment with me. At twenty-three, I quit my sales job in New York City to become a yoga teacher and officially embark on my entrepreneurial journey. Many would think, "you are crazy, why would you leave your comfortable position with benefits?"

But I think what most people do not realize is, "what is the purpose of life without health, wellbeing and inner fulfillment?" No amount of 401k benefits or kegs at the office or great happy hours with my team could sway me from living as a shell of my existence to simply "stay the course" that society prescribes.

Reclaiming who we are makes others uncomfortable because they have to sit face to face with their own life. It's easier for them to judge those who choose their own path and reclaim their power than allow themselves the same sense of freedom to leave, and leave swiftly, whatever is not truly for them.

I think back to one of my research papers in high school on how standard tests were the worst indicator of true intelligence. It's as if young me knew that we were so much more intelligent than what the filling out of small little bubbles with the perfect Ticonderoga 2 pencil on a test would tell us we were. If you think about it, the standard education system, the one which I was brought up in, says, "you must learn this one way and take these standardized tests to get good grades to go to the best school to get the best job to buy a nice house to support your family."

Well then, why are people dealing with mental health issues more than ever today?

Why do people look like zombies as they get on public transport to go to the job that they hate for 60% of their waking hours?

Why are people dealing with chronic health issues more than ever?

Why are the "leaders" of this world creating rules for people that don't honor the people?

Our society is in a crumbling space. The systems are no longer sturdy.

I remember when my Kundalini yoga teacher began to teach about the age of Aquarius, which is focused on massive advancements in technology, heart-centered leadership, sovereignty and personal responsibility. It was as if these lightbulbs began going off inside me. Yes, yes, yes!

The age of Aquarius is a time in history where we are leaving the hierarchical structures that said government, religion and people had rulership over us—structures that this world was built on. We were taught to look up to these governing figures, but as consciousness evolves and technology advances, more and more people are realizing these structures were put in place for ordinance and obedience, not creative freedom or personal responsibility. We cast our burdens, troubles and questions on these authority structures, looking for a savior. Right now, the power is coming back to the people and many are beginning to ask vital questions.

"Does it have to be this way?"

"Do we have to live and follow what others have done?"

"Can we create our path and forge on?"

People are beginning to question the way things have been. The way they were raised. The beliefs they've accepted as true. The leaders they once believed and trusted. The ways of society.

"We cannot solve our problems with the same thinking we used when we created them."
- Albert Einstein

For so long, problems, disease, and even talk therapy have been focused on the same linear thinking that started the problem.

What we are moving into is that more and more people are expanding their consciousness to move beyond the problem and sit into the unlimited potential solutions.

INVITATION

I always like to think of books as invitations to expand our perspectives. So many books in my own life have done that for me, like *Autobiography of a Yogi* by Paramahansa Yogananda, *Frequency* by Penney Pierce, and *Think and Grow Rich* by Napoleon Hill, just to name a few.

I'm sure those who read these words and engulf this book will have a similar experience. You will be able to reflect on your own life and think about the beliefs you've accepted as true. The first step is always awareness, right?

When it comes to these changing and shifting times, as systems collapse in front of our eyes, we face questions, thoughts, and a whole slew of emotions.

Maybe we are grieving the death of the old ways.

Maybe we are starting to ask some questions.

How do I want to live my life?
How do I want to *lead* my life?
Who am I?
What do I believe to be true?
What are my values?
How am I ready to lead in new ways?
How will I navigate forging a new path?
Am I ready to go first?
Who will walk beside me?
What is my message to humanity?
What can my actions as a leader remind them of?

For me, sitting with my answers to the above questions is non-negotiable at this point. I am even feeling some sense of urgency as I write this chapter to you all.

We must be willing to ask challenging questions and go first as leaders of the future.

FUTURE OF LEADERSHIP

In my eyes, the leaders walk among us now. In my eyes, the leaders of the future will not have all the degrees or letters after their name. They will not be the religious figureheads or the presidents; the leaders of the future will be you and I.

People who thought differently.

People who believed in personal responsibility.
People who believed in empowerment.
People who remind others they can be and live their life however they so choose.

We are seeing this play out in front of our eyes right now. The people are standing up for their values. They are leaving their jobs because their morals, values and beliefs are not in alignment with that of the organization or job they have been at for years, even decades.

Years ago, I didn't know what to call my ideal client. I spoke to them as people who wanted to be the leaders of their life, and I see this coming to fruition now more than ever.

You don't need to have a six-and seven-figure business to be a leader.
You don't need to be a corporate executive to be a leader.
You don't need to be a government official to be a leader.

You could be a mom, a friend, an entrepreneur, a co-worker.
And you can decide exactly who you are, who you want to be, what you believe in, what matters most to you and you get the choice to hold yourself to it.

No one outside of you can take your power away unless you let them.

As consciousness evolves, more people become aware of what they are consuming. As sensitivity on the planet rises, there is this deeper understanding of the information, relationships and intentions people, especially leaders, allow in their field. Media, TV, News, Podcasts, Music, Conversations, Food. It all matters.

And the leaders of the future world know this to be true. They understand the interconnectivity of everything in their lives and hold themselves to their beliefs of what is true for them. They listen to the inner nudges of their soul. They act upon the whispers before they become screams. They release friendships, relationships and even connections that don't leave them feeling more vibrant and radiant than when the conversations began. They go first and forge into unknown lands of the mind and the heart. They walk paths never before walked, hand in hand.

CLOSING THOUGHTS

As I sit here, writing this, I feel excited and proud to be speaking about this topic right now in history. I can make sense of all the times in my life that I ventured down the path less known or was unwilling to compromise my health or wellbeing. Quitting the jobs, leaving the relationships, pivoting my business, saying no to sh*t food that was laden with chemicals, bringing my own meals to family dinners to honor my health, letting go of friendships that didn't light me up or align with my future.

It was all Divine. It was all perfect.

Leadership is something I feel I was born for.

The first of three children.

Born on the first of the month to entrepreneurial parents.

Going first is in my nature.

But that doesn't mean it's always easy.

Always remember, you are never alone on this journey.

I am with you.

God is with you.

Leaders, we've got this.

ABOUT THE AUTHOR

Bridget Aileen Sicsko is the founder of Exalted Publishing House, a podcast host and a visibility coach. She helps successful entrepreneurs stand out and be featured as leaders in their industry by sharing powerful stories, writing best-selling books and gaining global recognition. Bridget believes in the power of words, stories and voices to shift our view of reality, our potential and our purpose on the planet. In addition, she considers herself a master community builder and has gathered hundreds of female leaders in her online community, mastermind program, networking events, and women's circles. Bridget also hosts a podcast, The Gathering MVMT, where she has interviewed over sixty entrepreneurs, TEDx speakers, authors, thought-leaders, and visionaries to discuss success consciousness, leadership, kundalini yoga, energetics, and quantum reality. Bridget has been featured in Authority Magazine, Women's Business Daily, Thrive Global, The Medium, on Ticker News, News 12 New York and several podcasts. She lives in New Jersey with her husband and her border collie beagle, Finn.

Website: *www.bridgetaileen.com*
Email: *bridget@bridgetaileen.com*
Facebook: *www.facebook.com/groups/rockthemiconline*
Discord: *www.discord.gg/eqkFw74sNC*
Instagram: *www.instagram.com/blissfulbridget*
Podcast: *www.podcasts.apple.com/us/podcast/the-gathering-mvmt/id1546684870*

3

CJ & MELISA KEENAN

INTIMACY AS A WAY OF BEING, VITAL KEYS TO THE GOLDEN AGE

A s you read this chapter—and the entire book—we always say, "don't take our word for anything." Instead, take a deep breath. Do it, right now. Soften, and allow your heart and mind to be open. Don't read from a 'check it out' perspective; read to find things that stir something within you, that speak to some deeper part of yourself. Things that speak to your truth, to your integrity, to your soul. If it is truly important for you in your life's journey, you will feel and know that it is good and true. This, after all, is lesson one of intimacy, or *into-me-see*: go within and feel. The answers about how you are meant to lead and thrive through the coming changes are all already within you; this book is simply meant to call those truths out of you.

ASLEEP AND BROKENHEARTED, BY MELISA:

> *"I have died every day waiting for you*
> *Darling, don't be afraid*
> *I have loved you for a thousand years*
> *I'll love you for a thousand more" - Christina Perri*

I was twenty-six years old, confused, abandoned and alone... my love, sleeping on the couch at his dad's house for months now, while I breastfed and changed diapers of all three of our children ages four and under, wondering where we went wrong. Against all my survival instincts, the advice of our parents and the furrowed brows of every college professor we studied under from that time forth... I had flung myself, open-heartedly and unabashedly, into a marriage with a man (boy) at ages twenty and twenty-two. We had both waited to have sex until marriage, following the tradition of our faith. We belong to a beautiful faith, and the teachings on family and marriage are unparalleled. You see, when you are married, in this faith, the officiator doesn't say, "You are now married until death do you part." Instead, he says, "You are now sealed, for time, and all eternity," in a special ceremony held in the temple which we believe is the literal House of The Lord. With that kind of insurance, surely our marriage would survive.

And yet here we were, broken down and destitute, the marriage dangling from a thread, and my whole world seemingly crashing down on top of me while my three babies look up to me to let them know that everything is going to be alright.

I will not share many of the details of what we faced during that time simply because the world does not comprehend or respect someone who has faced their own demons. But suffice it to say, there were lies and betrayal, and I was completely traumatized.

Marriage can be like that, can't it? So high, and so low, so exquisite, and so tense, deep pleasure, and often deep pain.

So, go with me as I take you a little deeper into our wedding day. Picture this; a shiny newly shaven twenty-two-year-old in his best suit and tie. A bright twenty-year-old me, radiant long black curly locks over the stark contrast of my white frilly dress that had layers upon layers of ruffles, both of us kneeling across the wedding altar. I had no family present in the room, and it didn't matter one bit. In that moment, all that mattered were his steel-blue eyes locked into mine and my tear-stained cheeks that ached from smiling so big. The officiator took a pause to tell us that the spirits of our children were also there, their hands on top of ours. My heart was soaring.

Then, those first sacred moments of physical intimacy on our wedding night; awkward, giggly and apprehensive, yet unable to hold back… I felt like I had waited an eternity for him to be inside of me.

Then, fast forward to the awe and wonder I felt as I received his full support delivering and welcoming our first little one to earth. Everyone told me he was squeamish and would probably need to leave the room, but he wasn't what everyone said. Instead, he was there with me covered in sweat, blood and tears.

The paradox of the highs and lows of marriage can feel so intense at times. It is what literally leaves us with a broken heart. As if both narratives running in our memory create so much friction like a tug-of-war that finally, if it gets too extreme, something happens and our heart just tears into two.

SKELETONS, BY CJ:

We all have skeletons, and I don't just mean the literal ones. Melisa mentioned it in her opening, without going into detail (that would be an entire book itself). We have learned that few people are willing to talk about the ones we figuratively keep in our closets. Our culture doesn't really lend itself to sharing some of the deepest, darkest, biggest challenges we face. It makes for a good movie to have someone go through a terrible past trial then quickly move to the end, where we feel good and experience that resolution. Most people don't like the reality though. You know the one that I am talking about—it's probably what you would refer to as your everyday life. Where we sit in the challenges and experience them for more than just thirty minutes before finding that resolution. We have all felt "stuck" with trials, weaknesses and consequences, many from our own decisions.

Melisa and I write these things to let you know that no matter where you are at, there is hope. No matter how big your figurative closet may be, despite the number of "skeletons" you may have, there is hope. No matter what you believe is coming or happening in the future, there is hope. Our own pits of despair and darkness have consisted of things like being on food stamps, Medicaid and feeling desperate with money, lying to Melisa about what I was doing or where I was, feeling like I couldn't reveal how I was wasting my time. I thought I was doing all the right things to preserve my marriage and being the best I could be at the time. We have hurt each other so much, and yet, we have also been the greatest source of joy for each other. What took us years of struggle we now help others achieve quickly. We write from a new vantage point that we once felt was impossible.

PARADOX, BY MELISA:

After about two and a half years of struggling to mend our relationship, I can distinctly remember looking over at CJ and both of us saying, "We never knew this kind of connection existed. We have to tell people about this." The connection we had created felt like nothing either of us had ever experienced. The healing we both accessed within ourselves, and for our marriage, gave us a renewed sense of what is really possible in this life. It is so beautiful.

But so many of us have been hurt so deeply that we cannot see the light and now entirely reject the concept of marriage and commitment in romantic relationships. Because I now teach globally about the beauty of marriage, women in droves have said to me, "Happy marriages are just a fairy tale, it isn't real," and "good luck selling handcuffs to the free." In our present day, so many have sunken into a dismal resignation, half-dead, wholly asleep. The world provides us with plenty of distractions and numbing chambers to lock away our souls, and the temptations prey on those who are simply weary from their long barren journey. Those who are the most susceptible to succumbing to the loud but subtle lull, are those who have been the most wounded.

I am not judging my sisters; I am empathizing with you. Tears are welling in my eyes as I write these words. Are you one of those who have locked their hearts away and thrown away the key?

So many of us have endured so much in our relationships. On the outside, we are tougher than nails and stronger than steel, but on the inside, we are bone-weary travelers, our hands and faces dirty and marred.

We didn't mean to lock our hearts away, but it seemed like the only option.

We don't mean to get caught up in the noise of society, and the distractions of the world. We aren't 'sinning', we are just seeking reprieve, seeking solace. So we get caught up in our work, the next promotion, distracted by the noise, the sales, the new cars, the botox, and the tangible things that help validate our existence. We forget why we started our businesses in the first place, or why we wanted to marry or have children in the first place. We show up in our marriages with contempt, feeling like the whole world is on our shoulders. We think, as women, that we have to be the heart and soul and the bronze and brains. "Do it all, and never let them see you sweat," are our marching orders. 'Business mode' just spills over into every aspect of our lives and it feels like we have to be "on" 24/7. It's a tangled up mess of energy confusion, role confusion, false identities and conditioning that has been plopped into our laps. Add pain to the mix and it can feel hopeless.

And yet, everything can be mended. Our hearts can become so big that the extreme opposites of life don't have to cause it to rip. We can encompass it all if we feel it is really worth it. In fact, our ability to internally hold paradoxes is directly tied to our ability to grow and progress to our fullest potential. Marriage provides a mirror of sacred healing; if we will be courageous enough to look, and keep looking, we will refine our very soul.

Committing yourself to being your best and creating the best marriage will provide the only sure and sturdy building blocks of society. It will provide that kind of home and stability for your children. It will even allow you to be the leader you are meant to be in your community. But committing to yourself and your marriage will also allow you to continue to listen to that little voice inside that says you want someone to do life with. It will allow you to experience the fullness of your birthright on the planet. It means you commit yourself to living a life of healing, transmuting all past ailments and the garbage of your DNA and ancestry, and ultimately experience total bliss within yourself and your marriage, regardless of the circumstances going on outside.

DOING IT ALL, BY CJ:

Melisa and I understand the difficulties businesspersons with families face today. Women are expected to be and bear it all. They are expected to compete with men in all areas of life and even expected to do it better, just like the old adage, "Anything you can do I can do better!" How can anyone live up to these expectations? The truth is, you are already doing it! You are already enough. You don't need to keep comparing yourself to someone else to determine what success is.

The same goes for men! We grew up hearing things like, "suck it up!", "don't be a pussy" or "get over it"... all these things that tell us to just move past our feelings and emotions. We learn from experts like Brene Brown and Tony Robbins that vulnerability, emotions and courage are what produce the best of everything and that goes for men too. Do you want more profit in your company, a better marriage and relationships, to be more connected to God or even have the best body of your life? Then, you have to stop listening to the old ways of thinking and start taking action on the most important things, like being authentic and vulnerable.

Melisa and I have a perfect life—we really have it all! Arriving where we are has not happened overnight, nor has it ended at this point. We live in the same world as you, with the expectations and pressures yet we know we'll never be perfect in this life. Knowing, accepting and living within this paradox allows us to communicate more effectively and forgive more quickly, creating deeper intimacy. It is what turns our epic adventure with unseen twists and loops into living our fairytale ending.

THE MAGIC OF POSSIBILITY, BY MELISA:

> *The mystery of marriage is great. Without it, the world would not exist. The existence of the world depends on people, and the existence of people depends on marriage. Then think of the power of pure intercourse, though its image is defiled.*
> *- The Gospel of Philip Section 64 & 65*

Society has us always looking outside of ourselves for our answers, but the feminine calls us and lures us to look inward. In a strong marriage fed a steady diet of deep, true, and raw intimacy, we are fully seen, known, and cherished by our partner and by ourselves. This is the reality of true intimacy or into-me-see. We first deeply see into ourselves, fully present, loving and accepting what is there. From this place, we are now open and can invite another in, to see us. It happens almost naturally and without force. It creates this space of open sharing, giving and receiving. A dance of masculine and feminine flows like our souls are literally dancing with one another even as our bodies dance with each other. From here, we are now capable of holding that space to deeply see into one another. And this is a moment by moment practice, one that benefits us whether single and dating or even in a marriage of over thirty years. How could you personally benefit from deeper intimacy in your life?

From this place of true intimacy, we begin to access magic and unlimited possibilities. We can access the elements to manifest and co-create our reality with our partners. In fact, we already are doing this unconsciously, and getting mostly mediocre results. But what if you did this consciously? What if we all woke up to the power that exists when two sovereign and intimate individuals come together spiritually, physically, mentally and emotionally in a sacred and holy marriage? Both individuals awake to their divinity and actively pursue to better the planet, making a happy and safe home for their children, and radiating their essence across the globe; she, in her divine feminine and he, in his divine masculine. How amazing could it be? What kind of influence could a couple like that have?

This is what I believe the couples will be like in the Golden Age.

From a passage I wrote not too long ago, I invite you to feel your way through these words as we explore what is possible. Sex is meant to be a sacred co-creation, nothing like what we have seen in our day to day current society.

The Universe is Asking You, "How much pleasure can you possibly stand?"

Laying in bed, her heart dreams it up, and it puts a smile across her lips.
She can feel a stirring within and the more she contemplates their next level, her
heart feels like it's going to burst and her desire expands and swells.
She's ready for the next level in her marriage.
So she opens up, in her mind, her emotions, her body, even her soul...
Wide. Wet. Ready. She invites him in.
Not just into her, into her sacred chamber. Then, into and through the portal that
she has just become.
They enter together.
Farther upward is only ever further inward.
And together they heal, together they forgive, together they expand... the quantum
leap has already begun. Time has already collapsed.
Welcome to heaven on earth.

Do you know what this feels like?

THE SACRED MASCULINE, BY CJ:

The passage written before this, by Melisa, is a total turn on! This is something that all men want to hear and have. It is a deep desire ingrained within both men and women, to have that incredible connection that surpasses what we know or even could imagine. How do we get there though? What do you do to take things to that next level?

It would be nice if there was a manual or simple video we could watch to get the answers we want or even feel like we need, but there isn't. This is where the power of the masculine comes into play. Men believe that women are unpredictable, or that they never know what they want. If you ask a married man why their wife is mad, or why she feels disconnected or whatever else it may be, they just shrug their shoulders and say, "I dunno." However, if a man takes just a few moments to reflect and really think about it, eight out of ten times they know exactly why she feels that way. The other two out of ten, she still knows, so just ask!!! As men, we fail to trust ourselves and lead the relationship because it requires diving into that emotional stuff and this may show that we are weak. We imagine the worst possible scenario is that we know what is wrong, but we might not be able to fix it. However, the most masculine thing that I can do is create and hold a space for my wife to have her feelings and express herself. I don't need to fix it all, especially not my spouse, she's not broken. As men, we need to stop acting like we don't know what women want and start stepping into the role we were really meant to play as leaders in our relationships.

Everything must burn...

The superiority of human beings is not apparent to the eye but lies
in what is hidden.
- The Gospel of Philip, Section 64

Our society praises and revere's only what we can see, what is tangible and visible on the outside of a person. Wealth, infrastructure, status, and who one associates with, typically determine what makes someone worthy of being venerated and followed. The systems, structures and institutions backed by the most wealth, win. This is how we align ourselves with the leaders that we then venerate and strive to be like, but it is based only on the surface.

Similarly, the way we, as a society, have done the institution of marriage is all wrong, all surface level. Even the ones that have endured through time. Simply having a long marriage doesn't make a strong marriage.

But everything is quantum, massively, fast-changing. Most of the structures, systems and institutions we currently subscribe to will not stand. Then, all that will remain to save society and create a new and bright reality is true and intimate marriages. This is because marriage as an institution, the main building block for society, and has the potential to bring the depth that we all crave.

Just as everything must burn on the outside, in the world around us, this is the time to allow the fire to burn within us as well. To burn up the impurities in our inner world like a great unveiling of all as it truly is. Our insides become our outsides. In the coming days, our leaders will not be able to lead by what is on the outside because we will be able to see and feel what is on the inside. And those who are in positions of leadership will only be those whose insides are worthy of being followed.

When our insides become our outsides, what will people see in you?

Your marriage and relationships are already begging you to reveal what is inside of you. Marriage is your training ground. You are a God or Goddess in embryo, and marriage is the womb.

Our insides; values, families, relationships, how we have treated people and ourselves, what we believe in and how far we have been willing to go to defend and cling to and BE in that belief, will be felt and sensed by all around us. It will be a society of leaders who be, rather than do, and who we can deeply connect and resonate with because there are no barriers to intimacy or 'into-me-see' with them and their spirits.

What still remains hidden inside of you? What rock remains unturned? Where are you living out of alignment with the reality of who you really are? If you aren't sure, then ask yourself, "what makes me feel really vulnerable?" and go there. This work is vital for our journey into the Golden Age, and it is vital to strong marriages with true intimacy as their foundation.

THE SILVER BULLET, BY CJ:

We inherently know that there is no "silver bullet" for the biggest challenges. The most satisfying results and rewards we receive in life never come from doing just one thing. It is a combination of things. Gold medalists do more than just practice their events, they do strength training, hone their diets and so much more. It is the same for the happiest people in life. We don't just do one thing, there isn't just one thing that will solve our problems. Finding answers and acting on them is a process. Unfortunately, a lot of people don't get to where they want to be, but why? What keeps people from getting there?

Pain. That's it.

It feels so much better and easier to numb out. Many of us don't even realize what we're doing, just avoiding pain. Reviewing my own life, it's almost shocking to see how much time I spent taking action to avoid pain, rather than pursue what I really wanted. You think you are different from the rest of us? Then, get real honest about why you haven't gotten to where you want to be. Inevitably, we can trace it back to you avoiding feelings of discomfort. It's crazy to think that there isn't a silver bullet for success but there seems to be one for failure; it's remaining unconscious to how much of your life is spent avoiding pain.

THE NEXT LEVEL, BY CJ:

There are a lot of different strategies we can use to overcome the discomfort and pain that keeps us from becoming our best selves. Melisa and I have transformed our marriage into a scaling machine. It's like a dream come true. What is your marriage doing for you? The closest comparison I have for what we experience is advertising; you put $1 in and get $10 out! If you aren't married yet, find that right someone you can create this with. If you've done all you can to recover your current marriage and it is not salvageable, don't stay. Do whatever you can to create this kind of marriage, you deserve it. This is how we've come to live our lives and know that it will exponentially increase our success and happiness, as we define them. It creates a foundation that puts us and the rest of the world into a higher realm of living. A step closer to that golden age, which is a place of expansion that accelerates us into our truest and highest selves, our God-like selves.

CREATING MARRIAGES THAT SHINE IN THE GOLDEN AGE, BY MELISA:

"Heaven on Earth is a choice you must make, not a place you must find."
- Wayne Dyer

So many people have studied the patterns that create amazing marriages and then written libraries full of steps and how-tos. I am grateful for their work, but I find a flaw in this whole approach.

If true divinity is at the core of who we really are, and marriage is a pattern of God, then our best marriage will come to us by listening within. The best path to your best marriage can only be crafted and birthed by the two of you, in your partnership. Not by the patterns and formulas recommended by the latest experts.

The first I ever sat down with a couple in my couples coaching program, I was amazed at what I saw. It was like I was looking at three individuals, not two. I saw the husband, the wife, and a third entity, which I have given the title, the Soul of the Marriage. It was just as vibrant, just as clearly there. It was almost tangible, with a personality, needs and desires. It would indicate where it had been in want for a long time, where it felt tension or staleness, or where it felt full and complete. The Soul of the Marriage was directly connected to the essence or spirit of both individuals in the marriage which connected and united the individuals in deep, binding and beautiful ways.

There is an energetic channel there that we can access at any time, by feeling within. Intimacy, or into-me-see as we describe it, starts with first understanding what you are sensing and feeling as an individual, and what those feelings indicate about what you deeply value. Then sharing that and reciprocally seeking to understand that in your partner. This is how the two of you can literally transcend together.

The Golden Age is full of beauty and glory. It is full of people of integrity, who wear their insides on their outsides and we love what we see. It is full of people who refuse to settle for less than the reality of their own divinity, who serve and bless and conduct miracles. And these people are connected in marriages and families that are happy, where intimacy is sacred, where true companionship and unity are commonplace and feel like the greatest pleasure you can possibly stand. It's pure and true and good and safe and it starts right inside of the walls of your home, today. You want the Golden age? You want Zion? You want your mind, body and spirit to change in the "twinkling of an eye," (1 Corinthians 15:51, Holy Bible) to have the peace, the abundance, the healing and all you could ever want for? It starts now, and it begins with intimacy as a way of being. It starts inside of us, when we decide to stop living complacent lives and staying complacent in our love and marriages.

The Golden Age starts when you say it starts, in your inner-vessel, in your marriage, and in your home.

CLOSING, WITH CJ & MELISA:

If we can allow our hearts to open and expand, then we can see the possibilities for how exquisite marriage actually can be. The reality is that strong committed relationships, marriages, are the vital building blocks of society; homes as sanctuaries, with a mother and a father, feeling safe and secure in their family when they don't have safety and security in the world around them, wives trusting their husbands and themselves, radiating from the inside out, husbands, confident, caring and intuitively connected. We need families gathered around the fire and the dinner table, talking about what really matters and eating food cooked with love, not stress, struggle and overwhelm. We need power couples raising conscious children, who are aware of their gifts and zone-of-genius at young ages and able to contribute and feel like an important and necessary member of the family, and then of society. We need marriages where both partners have a vision for themselves, their family, and for our communities and societies and want to progress and serve at the same time, lifting our fellow brothers and sisters while lifting ourselves.

As you embark on this journey, have patience with yourself and your loved ones. This doesn't happen overnight—it didn't happen overnight for us either. There are amazing people with amazing marriages out there who have their hands outstretched to help you up. Just remember, no one outside of you will ever know your heart, or your relationship better than you. You, in your truest intuition, know what you most need. So as you seek guidance, and DO SEEK GUIDANCE, look for those who will help you remember the wisdom inside of you.

When in doubt, dance. Let your walls down. Open yourself to give and receive wonderful passionate sex together. Do something wild you haven't done before. Be real, be bold, be vulnerable. Act on your hope and faith. Take a risk and jump in. Try, and then try again. Let the feminine keep you wide open, playful, wet and ready, sacred and sovereign. Let the masculine lead, strengthen, hold and make stable and penetrate to the core. Let no part be hidden.

This is how true intimacy will lead us into the Golden Age.

27

ABOUT THE AUTHOR

CJ and Melisa Keenan are CFO and CEO of an international intimacy coaching company helping the top 1% learn to access polarity in marriages and relationships through their feminine and masculine power to create intimacy that transcends. Melisa is a USA Today bestselling author and keynote speaker and the go-to expert on intuitive relationships serving the heart of the high-profile businesswoman to experience pleasure, through the feminine, without limits. CJ received his M. Ed. in Educational Leadership and has led the coming generation through education for the last six years. He is skilled at helping men tap into their sacred masculine to lead more fully in their lives and relationships to create more of what they want. Their family of six love to garden and play on their hobby ranch in Northern Nevada and love to adventure and explore the world.

Get your free intimacy guide: *www.melisakeenan.com*
Email: *support@melisakeenan.com*

4

DR. KRISTINA TICKLER WELSOME

A NEW MEDICINE WOMAN

We see that our world is changing. We know that we want and need to change as well. Yet we may not know exactly how that should happen. The process of 'becoming' often starts with a process of unbecoming all the things you were taught or that you thought you had to be. This is a shedding of your old skin and your old self. Releasing the past. Letting go of who you thought you were, to make space for the person you are becoming.

A time to make space for new things that are coming to you, to see old things through a new lens, so that you have space for inspiration and creativity, growth and development, change and a new way of doing life. It's not easy to let go of what is familiar, comfortable, and known. However, ease may need to be surrendered in order to turn our face to the sun arising in this new dawn and embrace the unknown, the unfamiliar and all that we desire our future to be. We will need to muster up the courage to face our fears, to dig deep for the faith to believe that all things are possible.

We will need to actively co-create this new experience for ourselves in connection and collaboration with other like-minded and heart-centered individuals. We can't sit passively and watch as the new world is created. To do so would likely mean your values and needs will not be considered or included, it will not be as you desire it to be, and you won't feel any sense of partnership for what is created.

LIMINAL SPACE

The liminal space is the space in between, the space between where we once were and what we know, and where we are going and what is unknown. Before you can hear what you are meant to know, you will need to get quiet and turn inwards for the answers that lie deep within. Acknowledge that your inner knowing and prior life experience is trying to show you that you are meant for something more. Embrace what you are being asked to do and willingly show up authentically as who you are inherently supposed to be. I see that the world is changing. Change of all kinds is inevitable. In this unbecoming of all the things that we are not, we release all of the burdens that are not ours to carry. We may need to shed our old skin as we determine who it is we aspire to be.

This is a time and space where we need not feel rushed, where we need to slow down or even pause completely. This is a good time for reflection. We can get so carried away with the hustle and bustle of life that we run from one thing to the next without thinking. It's necessary to truly connect with ourselves so that we can reflect and consider what has been working for us in the past that we want to keep and bring forward, as well as discard the things that are no longer helpful or useful. We may not know what needs to be added in until we take action and start to move forward. As we discover who we are, we may be more easily able to ascertain what more is needed in the world.

While I have ideas of who I am and want to become, I still struggle at times to release my past, face my fear of the unknown, and embrace how it will all unfold. It feels disingenuous for me to pretend to have the answers when I simply don't...yet. But I believe I will. I look forward to the day when the knowing comes to me. Until then, I wait in this liminal space, with full faith that the story will unfold in divine timing as it should. And that I will rise to meet the challenge as I always have in my past.

PERMISSION TO SPEAK THE AUTHENTIC TRUTH IN FREEDOM

Unleashed. I know it's time to be free of the chains that have bound me. Finally let off the leash, a chain has been removed and I am free to roam about life and the world. I'm free to explore. I'm free to be me. I'm not tethered by any restrictions, by anyone else's expectations of who I am. My heart, mind, body, and soul now have permission to follow my life's calling to be exactly who I was meant to be. Who I was born to be. To embrace my unique gifts, talents, and purpose in this world to show up as love and to be loved. And to teach others to do the same. To release the walls of domestication that society has taught me to live within my entire life. The rules my parents set, the rules my church set, the rules that culture set—I am now free to create my own authentic agreements with myself about who I want to be and how I'm going to conduct myself. Permission has been granted.

Untamed. I know it's time to stop living in the domesticated way that I've been raised to and instead embrace being wild, free, and liberated. I'm not willing to hide and be invisible any longer. I'm not going to continue living my default story of "I'm nothing", because not only am I some-thing...I'm something special. I am going to take a stand for living an authentic life that I love, full of abundance, health and filled with fierce joy. In living this way I will courageously lead by example and allow others to choose the same. By making this stand I can create a bigger impact. By sharing what I have experienced and learned, I can help others give themselves permission to take the gag off, to remove the mask they wear, to show up as who they truly are without feeling censored by their parents, their siblings, their loved ones, and society. It is time for me to stand securely in my own authentic truth.

Uncensored. I know it's time to stop censoring the thoughts in my head, and the feelings in my body. The time has come for me to trust the intuition I feel deep down in my soul. I know it's time for me to stop staying quiet. It's time for me to speak up and use my voice to proclaim whatever it is that I want and need to say. I take full ownership of the fact that while nobody ever explicitly told me to be quiet or stay small, it's still a sense that I got from the world around me that I should be quiet and keep my thoughts and emotions to myself so no one else had to hear, deal with, or comfort me. While not officially censored, I recognize I need to allow myself permission to speak. I don't need to wait to be invited, encouraged, or forced to share what it is that I'm thinking, feeling, needing, or wanting from those around me. For me to be able to show up authentically, I must be able to communicate what's on my mind. This takes vulnerability, courage, and honesty. From my perspective and experience, I have found it's ultimately worth it to be able to share my thoughts with the people I love and cherish the most, to resolve conflict in my personal or professional life, or to spread my vision and message out loud and clear to the world.

INTEGRATED HOLISTIC WELLNESS AND HEALING

Here is what I know to be true, as both a healer and a woman who has had to do deep healing work. The way and manner in which we heal is as unique and variable as we are. For each of us to obtain the medicine we need to heal, we need to intuitively connect with what our body is crying out to us to provide it with. Often it is the body that is communicating our pain and suffering to us, but it often speaks out for our entire self. We need a holistic integration of all elements of our humanity—heart, mind, body, and soul—for each of us to become the best version of ourselves. To create and sustain genuine healthy relationships, achieve financial abundance, and pursue your deepest desires and passions, you need to be a whole and healthy human.

Thomas Jefferson was quoted as saying, "The doctor of the future will give no medicine, but will interest his patient in the care of the human frame, in diet and in the cause and prevention of disease." We live in a society where we buy life insurance that pays out when we die, we buy health insurance that kicks in when we're sick and have limited access to or fail to get in contact with the health care service we need to help us truly get to the root of our problems. The physical is treated while the mental and emotional source is ignored or goes untreated.

From the King James Bible, Luke 4:23, "And he said unto them, Ye will surely say unto me this proverb, Physician, heal thyself."

Maybe it is time to attend to our own wounds in preference to pointing out the faults of others. Being willing to look inwards and heal ourselves will allow each of us to show up in a more whole way in the world. If our own cup is full, we can then show up with the full capacity to give and replenish others.

I would that it was that easy. But actually, maybe it is. We are born with an inner knowing or an intuition, a connection with our heart, our mind, our body and soul that gets domesticated out of us, from the time we're born until the time that we get sick. We doubt what we innately and intuitively know to be true. Psychosomatic illnesses occur when our emotional state is intrinsically linked with our physical state. Yet we separate the body from the psyche and fail to integrate the treatment of an entire human being in need of care, love, and support. We fail to consider prevention, proactive measures, and maintenance of all parts of our being. We buy the brand new car of our dreams from a dealership and faithfully follow the prescribed maintenance schedule of oil changes, tire rotations, and checkups to make sure that this beautiful car stays beautiful and functioning well for us. Why do we not treat our most precious resource, the one beautiful body carrying our heart, mind, and soul that we were given at birth, with the same concept of care? Why do we not hydrate, nourish, move, explore, enjoy, and nurture it the way that we do everything else in our life? Take this time to pause and listen to the whisper that tells you of the needs your body yearns for.

NURTURE YOUR HUMAN NATURE

The field of genetics and epigenetics has been exploding in the last twenty years and offers us an opportunity to make lifestyle decisions that can integrally enhance and benefit our holistic wellness and limit or control both the communicable and non-communicable disease processes that might befall us. We tell ourselves the story that our nature is genetic - it's inherited, it comes from our family, and it can't be changed. That's just not true. It may be written in your genetic code. But that code is like an alphabet, with letters A through Z that you're born with. But as you've noticed as you type on your computer, fonts can be changed which make a simple letter A take on many different permutations, depending on if you decide to be fancy or casual. Our genetic expression can change depending on the choices you make—if you decide to be active or not, depending on if you decide to nourish it and let it be healthy or not. Epigenetics is the lifestyle that you choose to create which surrounds your genetic code. It intimately affects whether or not certain genes are turned on or off which is called expressed. So while we are born with our basic nature, we also get to choose how we nurture it. What is your human nature? More importantly, are you nurturing it?

How do you nurture the emotions that come up within your heart? Do you repress them? Do you suppress them? Do you deny them? Do you mock yourself for having them? Do you shut them down? You would be wise to allow yourself to connect with your body and feel. To encourage the feelings, translate them into emotional intelligence and use them as a message about how you're feeling and what you might need to do differently in your life. Learning to use this to guide the decisions and choices you make to ensure they are healthy and how to express your feelings to improve your relationships with others is helpful.

How do you nurture the thoughts that come into your mind? Are you aware that only five percent of your thoughts are actually conscious? The other ninety-five percent run in a subconscious replay track in an unconscious continuous loop in your head like Muzak at a local shopping store. There are unconscious and subconscious thoughts that you might not even be aware of, that maybe got implanted there in your early childhood, childhood, young adulthood, adult life, or even as recently as yesterday. Those subconscious thoughts that tell you, "I'm nothing. I'm not important. I'm not good enough. I'm not worthy." Those thoughts run around in your head 60,000 times a day. Do you want to choose to let them run amok? Or would you like to meet those thoughts and learn how to stop them and change them, so that the subconscious track always running in your mind is much more supportive of the life that you choose to have?

What's in your soul? Do you have a great purpose in life? Do you have a reason to get out of bed in the morning? Do you believe in God, the divine, the universe, mankind, or something else greater than yourself that helps guide you and drive you? That gives you hope and faith, and something to believe in when you're in this liminal space of not knowing where things are going. There's no right or wrong answer for the state of your spirituality. Studies show that having spirituality in your life can greatly impact and enhance your health and your recovery from disease, illness and injury, and certainly can give you meaning in your life and help support you on those dark days when you forget the reason you're here.

How are you nurturing your physical body? We need proper hydration, nutrition and quality food. We need adequate sleep, rest and recovery. We need to manage our stress and participate in regular aerobic, strength training and flexibility exercise. We often do these things because they're supported and encouraged by a culture that values fitness and attractive bodies. But what is your actual connection with your body? Do you appreciate the functions that it can do for you? Do you love the skin you're in? Are you in touch with your sensuality and your sexuality? Can you appreciate your assets and attributes? Do you have a love or hate relationship with your body? Remember that your body is the vehicle for your heart, mind, and soul to be carried in. So if you're not taking good care of that vehicle, then what's your internal self being carried around in? If your internal self isn't well, it's going to have an impact on the aches, pains, and tensions that you feel in your physical body.

A VISION FOR YOUR FUTURE WELL-BEING

The beautiful thing is that all these parts of us work hand in hand to enhance and support each other. The bad thing is when there's self-doubt, stress, fear, injury or trauma in any of those areas, they have a significant impact on the others as well. Your environmental surroundings play a huge part in how your heart, mind, body, and soul feel. I suggest that if you're not surrounding yourself with an environment that supports your growth and health and well-being, you consider changing that to nurture your nature in a more healthy manner.

Doing life can be hard, but also beautiful and joyful in so many amazing ways. I think we have to get comfortable with that, to embrace the fact that nothing is for certain, that nothing is guaranteed. That can be a scary place to sit and to wait, and sometimes lonely to simply be fully present with ourselves. Try to be at one with nature, to feel like more than simply a small speck in the vast universe but learn to be in harmony with the rest of mankind. All we can do is this, be secure in the knowledge we were born to be exactly who we are, and trust that the process will unfold in front of us, in due time. To have faith to continue believing in ourselves and in humanity, and in the world.

We are unleashed, untamed and uncensored in the liminal space. The space in between the space where we were and what we know, and where we are going and what is unknown. Courageously we follow our authentic desires and go forth into a truly new way of being human. Are you living your most authentic life? If not, I encourage you to find what is in your heart, mind, body, soul, relationships, environment, vocation or financial situation that is causing you to hold back. What causes you to limit yourself when there's no need. Your unique voice and message are needed as we create this new world, because they're different from mine. They're different from everyone else's. It has a value and a purpose. You should be living fully and out loud.

ABOUT THE AUTHOR

Dr. Kristina Tickler Welsome, DPT is a Doctor of Physical Therapy, Owner of The Key To Wellness and The Key Publishing, a Holistic Life Transformation Coach, and International Bestselling Author and Publisher. Decades of professional experience with patients, students, and clients makes her coaching effective, efficient, and easily integrated into your life. Her passion is to support the well-being and healing of your heart, mind, body, and soul as you learn to love your authentic self. Tina will empower you to become the author of your own life story as you discover unconsidered possibilities, remove barriers to success and unlock your full potential to live a creative life you love. Her own personal life journey prepared her to use her voice to amplify the voices of others to create even more impact in the world. You can find her enjoying living her best life as a mom of three divine masculine men in the making and expanding her own potential as a perfectly imperfect human being.

Website: www.thekeytowellness.net
Facebook: www.facebook.com/kristina.welsome
and www.facebook.com/thekeytowellness.net
and www.facebook.com/groups/soulnourishingconversations
Twitter: www.twitter.com/drtinawelsome
Instagram: www.instagram.com/thekeytowellness.tina
LinkedIn: www.linkedin.com/in/drkristinawelsome
Email: tina@thekeytowellness.net

5

DR. MELISSA WALKER

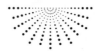

My story is that of the typical wounded healer. My body has experienced countless health issues for as long as I could remember. From asthma to migraines, various orthopedic issues, endometriosis, tremors, diabetes, ulcerative colitis and Crohn's disease—to say that I have been through a lot would be an understatement.

It's been eleven years since I made the full surrender to my soul's work which is for the highest good of all, and I'm excited to share with you some of the things that I have learned on this journey to wellness and wholeness.

When I had my soul awakening, I had been suffering from severe ulcerative colitis for over fifteen years, and I had been on high doses of steroids and immunosuppressive drugs to manage the debilitating symptoms of the colitis. I wasn't absorbing nutrients, so I was underweight, weak, constantly cold, and I spent most of the time in the bathroom with hemorrhagic diarrhea.

It was always bad, but it was even worse with stress. I was struggling to work just to have medical insurance coverage, my marriage was strained, and each day was filled with the anxiety of not being able to make it to the bathroom in time.

I had just been hired to be the medical director of a new veterinary hospital, but I had reached a low point where I knew that I couldn't go on. I had been strong for so long, but I reached my edge. I had to stop working. I had nothing left. I could feel my spirit leaving my body, and I knew that I was close to leaving this world.

Something overtook me, and I knew that my soul needed to be on the beach. Even though I was essentially bedridden, I needed to smell the saltwater, to feel the wind on my skin, and the sand under my feet. I needed to be closer to the mountains, my true love.

I gathered all the strength that I had, which wasn't much but just enough, and I got into my car, and I drove myself to Alki Beach in Seattle. My skeletal body slowly and gingerly made its way to a bench by the dark gray waters of Puget Sound.

I was thirty-two years old, but I moved like I was ninety. My previously strong and athletic body struggled just to walk the short distance from my car to the beach. At that moment, the bench was my Everest, and I moved by sheer will alone. I had arthritis in all of my joints, and my muscles had all but disappeared. Each movement brought tears to my eyes. I moved slowly but with purpose.

I sat there under an overcast sky looking over the Olympic mountains and had a conversation with God.

At first, I pleaded, "I just don't get it. I would do anything. I want to live." Tears rolled down my face. "I just don't get it; I've tried so hard." My feet were on the ground, but I could feel my spirit lifting up out of my body, like a balloon over the water.

I sat there, breathing in the salty air, and allowed my brain the space to rest, and I found my beating heart. She wanted to say something too, "I feel like I have so much to contribute to the world and there are so many things I want to do. There are so many places I want to go."

I felt myself dissolving into the landscape, my gray sallow skin perfectly matching my surroundings, and I realized I just couldn't fight anymore.

"I don't get it, but I guess if this was supposed to be my life, then so be it." Tears welled up in my eyes, and at that moment, I made peace with dying. It was pure and genuine surrender. There was nothing else to do.

Surrender wasn't something I contemplated, or that was familiar. It was quite the opposite. I had been fighting to survive my entire life, but in that moment, as I felt my life force drifting away, it was so natural, and so easy to surrender. It was almost autonomic, like an exhale.

I couldn't really make sense of it, but somehow, I had a sense that my soul was needed on another assignment, even though I thought that there was plenty to do right here, right now.

Surrender was quite the opposite of defeat, it was like yes, "I know I'm powerful and intelligent and loving, but maybe I need a different body to accomplish my soul's work." It was surrender for the highest good for all.

I genuinely didn't understand, but I just didn't have the strength to fight anymore. Clearly, I wasn't in control.

From that moment on, my whole world shifted, and as I began my trust in the universe, the divine, or what some may call God, I began to perceive my reality differently and began to accept the gifts that were always waiting for me.

A week after my surrender, my body, which was strengthened by my commitment to be an instrument for the highest good and by my desire to be the best doctor that I could be found itself at an all-day continuing education event learning about nutrition and whole food supplements.

It was at this event where I learned about muscle testing which is also known as applied kinesiology and how it is used to determine deficiencies, infections, and toxicities in the body. It is also used to determine what substances help restore balance and strength to the energy field. When this measurable energy field is strong, the body has its own innate capacity and ability to heal.

The following week I found myself at the office of a wonderful chiropractor, who performed these muscle tests. He was pressing down on my arm, and at times his assistant's arm while she was touching me (because I was too weak to maintain a muscle lock) to see which energies would make me weak or increase my energy field and make me strong.

At first, my mind was resistant, and my internal dialogue literally was "I can't believe that I'm paying for this" because I did not comprehend at the time what he was doing, but I had nothing to lose, so I went home and began taking the supplements and low and behold I actually felt better each time I took them.

They were helping me to detoxify heavy metals and to support my adrenal glands while providing me nutrition that my body could absorb and utilize. Feeling better motivated me to continue the treatment protocol. I had never felt better after taking medications, so this was a distinct improvement, and I was excited about the possibility that I was actually getting better.

As I began to improve, I realized that I had no idea of the physical pain that I had been living with because I had suppressed it in order to survive. My brain fog also cleared, and I recognized that I had been operating from significant diminished mental capacity despite still being high functioning in my work.

I became aware that there were millions of people just like me who had no idea that they were even compromised. That people are living in a state of survival without the remembrance of what it actually feels like to be well. I have deep compassion for others who are struggling in this way.

As my body began to heal, I began to make decisions about how I was living my life. My previously loving and supportive marriage had become unhealthy, and my partner was not shifting and growing in the same ways that I was. He could not see the progress that I was making, and he still saw me as "a sick person." I knew that I needed to move on from this relationship in order to completely heal. I had to give up a notion of a future with a person I still loved deeply, in order to take care of myself in the present moment and to allow myself the space to become a new version of myself instead of holding onto who I had been.

During this healing process, I discovered several healing modalities such as acupuncture, herbal medicine, homeopathy, chi nei tsang, and energy medicine and my inner knowing was that they were all more nourishing and healing than any synthetic medicine. I also practiced yoga and had awareness of my posture and breath.

I began to devour all information on holistic healing methods, and I started my own house call veterinary practice. I was able to have deeper connections with my patients and clients which was good for my soul, and I was amazed by the results that I was seeing with these ancient healing practices. I would even surprise myself with the successes, and it was heartwarming to know that I was making a real difference in the lives of others.

As I saw positive results in my practice, I began to learn about the sordid history of allopathic medicine and how the pharmaceutical industry dominants the educational system. The reality is that drugs are never developed to be a cure, but act as symptomatic band-aids (which can be helpful at times), but ultimately, they do not lead to healing, and oftentimes lead to side effects as they repress symptoms, in the way that we repress our emotions to survive. The only way to fully recover is to get to the root of the issue which is almost always toxicity of the physical, mental, emotional, and spiritual bodies. Once the toxicity is removed or transmuted, our bodies are fully capable of healing.

At first, I was quite angry with my previous doctors, the insurance companies, and the system at large for not being able to help me more in my time of need. This kept me in a spiral of anger and frustration that I had grown accustomed to, but over time, I realized that they were only doing the best they could with the knowledge that they had learned in school. I began to recognize that holding onto this anger and frustration was doing nothing productive and only hurting myself. In Chinese medicine, we know that the liver holds the feeling of anger and frustration and to fully detox, I needed to transmute these energies and let them go.

I was still dealing with depression from the loss of my marriage, leaving conventional medicine, lost friends, and my absent family and my soul called out to me to begin a journey of hiking part of the Pacific Crest Trail. The soul calling was loud and even though I couldn't really afford to take three months off from work and that I was afraid that I could lose the practice that I had taken so much time and energy to build, I could not ignore the call, so I put all of my belongings into storage and began the trek through Oregon with just a pack on my back.

This trip was both grounding and inspiring for me. I am energetically sensitive and being away from EMF and the constant demands for my energy and attention were healing for my nervous system. I was in deep commune with nature and the movement and beauty brought life back into my body. I was able to clear my mind and just be, which was incredibly healing. I began to regain confidence in my body and recognized that I felt better when I physically exerted myself. I have always been deeply connected to nature and my heart was communicating constantly with the trees, rivers, mountains, and rocks around me.

In addition to the colitis, I had also been experiencing full body tremors and balance issues since my first year of veterinary school and I thought that walking over many miles might be an effective way of rebalancing my body. Ultimately, this did not prove true, and I developed a stress fracture in my right foot.

My years of suppressing pain came in handy as I needed to walk twenty-two miles out of the woods with a fractured foot and a heavy backpack. I hitch-hiked to a Buddhist temple where I was taken in and was able to do meditations in the morning with the resident monk. The universe was giving me clear signals to meditate (this was not the first time), but at that point in my journey, I still wasn't able to calm my mind outside of these meetings with my beautiful teacher.

I returned back to Seattle without a home and was taken in by a friend. We became extremely close, extremely fast, and this relationship ended up in heartbreak. There was a situation that triggered this friend and she reacted out of deep unresolved pain which ultimately resulted in me being pushed out of a spiritual community. This event resulted in me developing severe frozen shoulder where I was incapacitated for over a year. I had no idea before this happened that an emotional injury could cause such a serious physical debilitation. I felt so alone in the world, and I wondered if I would ever find people who would love and accept me.

In retrospect, I realize that this was such a beautiful lesson for me to learn. Because of it, I read Gabor Mate's book, *When the Body Says No*, and I literally said to myself after nine months of extreme pain and disability, "Ok body, I'm not going to direct negative emotions toward you anymore," and just like that, the muscles that had been locked down in my shoulder completely relaxed and unwound. It was so profound for me to experience the results that such a simple heartfelt intention could have on my physical body. To understand that genuine love for the self could transform physical pain and disability in moments was a beautiful gift.

Despite all of my progress, I was still restless inside, and I still held a lot of resentment and hurt from my childhood and various traumas that I had experienced throughout my life that left me feeling powerless and unloved. I understood a lot intellectually, but I was still having difficulty putting it all into practice.

For many years, I was doing just fine. I was healthier than I had ever been in my body, but a few years ago, I had a flare-up of the ulcerative colitis and I wasn't responding to any treatments even though I had gained quite a bit of knowledge and success with treating my own patients and that I had access to world-class health care practitioners.

I was seeking healing outside of myself from master healers as well as with sacred plant medicine. While this was very helpful, in order to fully transform, I needed to learn how to control my mind and actually learn how to meditate.

I often find books when I'm ready for their message and during this time of quiet desperation, I read *Becoming Supernatural* by Joe Dispenza. It was time for me to go deeper into exploring my mind and beliefs. It was a clear message, and I was finally ready to receive it.

I ended up at a week-long meditation event, and my team leader immediately recognized my heart and persistence and on day two, I ended up telling my story in front of 900 people. Dr. Joe asked me what I was going to do when my body was better, and without skipping a beat I said, "I am going to do what you do, because I understand both the science and the spirituality." After I spoke, he turned off his mic and said to me that I needed to love myself as much as I love others.

I had no idea at the time, but he was giving me the secret to the deepest healing of my life.

All the love and appreciation that I was looking for outside of myself were actually available to me by me.

I now understand the fundamentals of quantum physics and that our thoughts and feelings create our reality and where we place our attention is where we place our energy. People had been telling me all along that I had a choice on how to think, feel, and be in the world, but previously I had always had an excuse about how difficult my life was, or a "you don't understand" rebuttal.

I understand now that we are eternal beings with a curriculum in this life, and we will continue to get the same lessons until we learn them. I had to learn boundaries, kindness to self, forgiveness, worthiness of abundance, and joy, while at the same time replacing judgment with acceptance, and embodying fearlessness. I open the door for you to do the same.

I began to recognize my negative self-talk and I would interrupt it and say something positive to myself which in the beginning felt quite hokey, but as I began to do this and embody gratitude for the things that I appreciated and that were going right, I began to see changes in how my life was unfolding and the people who I was attracting, and the synchronicities that were occurring.

Meditation, breathwork, movement, restful sleep (with a silk eye mask to reduce light pollution), dance, nourishing my body with organic whole foods, and a deep communion with nature are all essential in my personal process. I am eleven years away from taking any pharmaceutical drugs and I had been told by my doctors that I would be on them for the rest of my life.

By living my authentic truth, I have become part of a community of people who are willing to be with me in my wholeness, to celebrate my accomplishments, and to play with me in the world. I am surrounded by those who are loving and kind. People like me and you who dream of a world filled with love and wonder, and who are courageously authentic to themselves.

I continue to take care of others, but not at the expense of myself. I monitor my thoughts and if something is bothering me, I feel into it and ask why, what is the lesson here, what belief has caused this experience and is that belief even true or if it's just habitual.

Most of all, I listen to my intuition and my heart's desires even when and especially when they don't make logical sense. I have created my life to be a spiritual treasure hunt and it's exciting and fun, and at times painful. I welcome it all. The universe will always help you when you are true to yourself. It has never once let me down.

It's a beautiful thing to be alive on this planet and I know that the more that I take care of myself, the more positive impact I can have in this world.

I am here to lead by example, by facing my fears, by feeling my feelings, and to love all with an open heart. I am here to dive headfirst into the unknown, so that I may experience something new and be an instrument of change in the world.

Please know that you are worthy of love just because you exist. The path to true healing involves gracing yourself with the same love and compassion that you extend to others. You are worth it and your unique expression is beautiful beyond compare. I hold the intention that you fully embody it with love and peace in your heart.

ABOUT THE AUTHOR

Dr. Melissa Walker is an integrative holistic veterinarian living in Seattle, Washington. After a lifetime of chronic disease, she has taken a new path to healing and has healed her own body and countless others by embracing the eternal truths of nature and ancient healing traditions.

After a near-death experience, she drastically changed her diet and has traveled the world, learning various healing arts. She practices acupuncture, herbal medicine, and Chinese Veterinary Food therapy, among other modalities in a truly holistic integrative approach to heal the root cause of disease.

She has a deep spiritual practice, is a certified yoga teacher, and is passionate about the mind-body connection and the human-animal bond. Her passion is educating people on how to transform both their pets' and their own health from surviving to thriving.

Every day she strives for a greater connection with herself, her community, and her planet.

Website: *www.drmelissawalker.com and www.vvcseattle.com*
Facebook: *www.facebook.com/melissa.walker.54943600*
and www.facebook.com/Dr-Melissa-Walker-103053611337195
Instagram: *www.instagram.com/drmelissawalker*

6

JACQUELYN ATKINS

Is there a place on earth you feel a really strong connection with?

Perhaps you've been there. Perhaps you still hold the dream to visit this place. Maybe there are many places.

I've always found it fascinating that some locations in the world draw me enticingly, and others have never interested me.

I now realise that the earth calls us to certain places because that particular site is asking us for an energetic exchange. We're receiving some form of activation for our life path from that land, and we give our energetic footprint in return. This happens whether we are conscious of it or not.

I've had a gypsy spirit all my adult life, going to whichever land whispers tantalisingly to my heart.

I don't remember feeling this way as a child, and it wasn't until I was twenty-one that my heart felt pulled to foreign lands. As a child, I was certainly very connected to nature and animals, and I dreamed of living my adult life on a farm that was a combination of James Herriot's Yorkshire and Enid Blyton's Willow Farm. I was just unaware that those farms didn't exist on my continent!

Since England did play a huge role in my future, and I actually lived in

Yorkshire for a short time, perhaps I had heard that calling in my childhood after all.

For as soon as my intern year as a physiotherapist was over, I flew to England to begin a lifetime journey of connecting with sites around the earth.

Not that I viewed it this way at that time. I was simply a traveller wanting to visit as many places as possible. It's only been in the past twenty years since I've become aware of the nature of energy and our relationship with the earth that I've been able to look back at my earlier travels and understand the bigger picture of why I was drawn to the places I was.

I began that first trip in 1989 working in the beautiful countryside of the north of England, not knowing that I was near the home of my soulmate. Twenty-five years later, I'd explore and live on this land with him, but for now, I was leaving my energetic footprint.

In 1990, a journey around Europe triggered a health crisis. I began in Morocco before moving to Spain and the countries of western Europe. As I travelled, I became more unwell and was eventually hospitalised in Ireland, although they weren't able to find a diagnosis.

That put an end to my travels and I was too sick to return to work, so I came home to Australia only to discover that glandular fever was the mystery illness. I never quite trusted the Irish health system after that!

I've returned to many of those countries again, some of which hold a very powerful energy for me. I've since realised that energetically I was experiencing a deep cleansing on that first European journey. As I stood on the land, memories held in my energy body were being released, as though the land and I had a contract for that meeting.

Were they ancestral or past life memories? I don't know and I don't think it's important. Maybe it was even a collective memory that I was accessing and transmuting. I'm not sure that we can ever truly understand this at a mental level—unless perhaps you're a quantum physicist! We often feel the need to create a story around an energetic experience rather than simply follow our intuition and be present to what is.

Recovered and refinanced, I returned to England in 1992 to continue my journey. This time, I was living in London but was very drawn to

Africa, and I spent six weeks travelling from Kenya to Cape Town. A few months later, Africa called me back, although this time Egypt was my focus.

Now this was definitely a location that had planted seeds since my school days. I adored Egyptian history. When I arrived on that land, I knew it deeply; it felt like home. At this time I still knew nothing about energy or the esoteric nature of Ancient Egypt, but I loved every moment of my time there. Egypt made my heart sing.

In fact, after a scuba diving trip to the Red Sea, I was offered a job at the dive centre to train as a divemaster. All I had to do was go back to London, leave my job, pack my stuff and return. This land and I had work to do together!

But as it turned out, England was not yet ready to let me go. Before leaving for my trip, I'd arranged to go on a date with a guy after my holiday. Unfortunately for Egypt, I had a good time on that date, so the divemaster opportunity and reunification with Egypt was cancelled!

I've never been back to Egypt even though I often considered it, so I assume that the land and I exchanged what we needed to.

However, this was not the case with England. I stayed there until the final day of my visa—I'd managed to get four years out of a two-year working visa! I left with great sadness because I felt more connected to the land in England than I'd ever felt with Aussie soil, so of course, it would call me back.

I don't intend for this to be a travelogue so will not bore you with the details of the many other places I was drawn to in my twenties. What is more important is that I went wherever my heart led me. Or as I now realise, I went wherever the earth guided me and my heart simply listened and responded.

So how does the earth guide us?

As physical beings, we are made of the earth. In fact, we truly are one with the earth – as long as we stay connected to her. But our point of connection has been disrupted, resulting in many of us feeling separate from the earth. We tend to think we live on her but are not of her. This has been our conditioning.

And this is why we find ourselves disconnected from her guidance, her cycles and her abundance. We have everything we need; all we have to do is open up our connection point and allow ourselves to receive.

So what is the connection point?

It's the feet chakras on the balls of our feet. This is how we unite our energy body with the earth energy, but for many of us, those chakras are closed, or certainly very constricted. This makes it challenging for us to feel the guidance. When these are open and we allow ourselves to receive, the earth moves through us, guiding our steps.

The greater our connection to the earth's energy through these chakras, the greater our connection is to our intuition and to the earth's abundance.

But as my twenties drew to a close, I did not have this understanding. I returned home believing that it was time to settle down. So it was no surprise that I soon met my first husband, who is a very grounded, non-gypsy spirit, and in the following few years, our three angels were born.

My spiritual connection to the earth energy birthed with them.

Following my son's birth in 1997, I studied energy healing, and around this time my itchy feet returned. They were meant to have retired! This led us to sell our house, unsure of our next destination. I felt called to Perth, but the stars didn't align and so we didn't move there. Yet.

By the time my daughter was born in 2000, the land of northern NSW began calling me loudly. We moved in early 2002, just before the birth of our second daughter.

Words don't do justice to the peace I felt in my heart the day we arrived in Byron Shire. I'd come home, and it has remained my home base for twenty years. The land here speaks to me so strongly, and whenever I've tried to leave, it's pulled me back. Our time together is not yet complete.

The first couple of years were spent in great exploration of the nature spirits of the land, and for a short time, I even had a faerie shop! Circumstances forced us to leave in 2004 so I could complete my contract with the land in Perth. It was a tumultuous time in Perth but also a time of great connection with the earth spirits on the land there. I used to converse with the rose devas and this led to some thought-provoking writing about my soul lineage. However, after eight months, my soul was in distress and my feet itched to return to the land of Byron.

Back home again I strengthened my connection with the land as I moved into sound healing. I would sing to the land and could feel the energetic exchange between the earth and myself as the vibration moved between us. Connection with the earth energy became integral to my life. My three kids ended up having a 'traditional' Byron upbringing of talking with nature spirits, sounding before meals, hugging trees and going everywhere barefoot. I made sure their earth connection channel would always be clear!

However, it turns out that being married with young children does not silence the voice of the earth if she wants my energy in a particular place. The land of Europe had not yet finished with me, and she made the call in 2006.

It wasn't an easy thing to organise, but every part of me screamed that I had to join this journey through Templar initiation sites of Europe. There were seven sites connected to the chakras, and I would lead the throat chakra initiation at Notre Dame Cathedral in Paris.

That journey changed my life. I flew to Spain via London, and as I waited in transit at Heathrow, I saw my previous European life through a different lens. I had purged so many energies when I travelled through the land with the illness, and now I was back for the next leg of the journey—the activation.

We began in Santiago de Compostela, the base chakra. Unlike most people who walk the Camino and end in Santiago, we drove the Camino backwards across northern Spain and into France. It was not a traditional pilgrimage!

When we drove across the border into France, I burst into tears. I'd been to France on my first journey and had loved every moment. I'd always had a deep connection to the culture since learning French at school, but this was something more profound. It was as though the land was saying, "Welcome back. I know you." Once again, I had that feeling of being home, and if I had been able to see what the next few years would bring me on that land, I'd have understood why.

We wound our way along the Pyrenees to the mountain of Montsegur and the village of Rennes-le-Chateau in the Languedoc. These places were unbelievably powerful for me, bringing back many memories, as well as activating me to new experiences. My sounding at these sites took on a quality I'd not experienced before. I was truly happy here and somehow knew that this would be the first of many visits to this land.

Without going into detail about the whole trip, I experienced huge activations at many of the sacred sites we visited in France. I also had massive releases, sometimes sobbing for hours. At every site I would connect with the earth through sound, receiving visions and insights from the earth in exchange. It was a humbling experience.

The journey finished in Scotland at the crown chakra site of Roslin Chapel. By now I knew that it was a part of my soul mission to bring groups back to these places.

So in 2007, I returned to France to do a reconnaissance for the journey I'd lead in 2008.

This journey brought me much more than land connections. Within days of arriving, I met Mark at Rennes-le-Chateau. I felt immediately that he was my soul mate and we both knew our connection ran deep. It would be seven years before the timing was right for us to be in a relationship, and eight years before we took our vows on a mountain near Montsegur. We returned to this land often, believing that one day it would be our home.

In subsequent years, I led three journeys to Magdalene sacred sites in France. Although I planned to lead a journey in the UK, it didn't happen. However, Mark and I visited many of those sacred places together over the years, intrigued with the energy of the ley lines that ran beneath them.

In 2008, I took another journey to Uluru, the heart of Australia. That land had been calling me for many years, and my experience there was heart-opening in a very raw way. Connecting to the songlines of that land through sound, was one of the most powerful experiences I've ever had. It truly felt as though I was connecting to all the songlines (ley lines) around the earth from that one point. I think that the land around Uluru is the closest I've felt to being one with the earth.

In 2014, Mark and I realised we no longer wanted to be apart and decided to commit to the longest-distance relationship in the world! He lived in England, and I was in Australia. Of course, our first reunion was in France. I'd been back to Europe twice since our original meeting, sometimes visiting new sites (the Basque region had become a favourite), but always revisiting those places in the eastern Pyrenees that had captured me in 2006.

On that journey, Mark introduced me to the Catalonia region of Spain, and whether we were on the southern or the northern side of those eastern Pyrenees, we both felt truly at home. Together we connected with the earth energy, whether it was in a forest, a little chapel by the sea, or a cathedral in the mountains. Most churches are built on a powerful energy vortex, and we were not only drawn to the energy of the ley lines running beneath them but also the esoteric symbolism of the buildings.

We had many journeys to this region over the next couple of years, and then something shifted for both of us and we no longer felt the pull of this land. Was our exchange with the earth complete here?

Our attention was diverted to Ireland.

Although Mark is English, his heritage is Irish and he's always had a longing to live there. Our second trip together in 2014 had been to West Cork. This was the first time I'd returned to Ireland since my illness, and the land welcomed me very differently this time! I felt such a deep connection to the land and nature spirits. We had the most amazingly playful time there, and it was no surprise that when Mark decided to relocate from England to Ireland in 2018, our new home was close to where we stayed on this visit.

I feel so blessed that Mark and I are attracted to the same places and adore hanging out together on the land. We each have our own way of connecting with it, but that connection seems to be more powerful because of our togetherness.

I miss those amazing experiences with him.

In September 2019, after four months in Ireland, I returned to Australia because Mark had a premonition that I wouldn't be able to fly home soon.

We arranged to meet in Bali in February 2020 but that wasn't to be. He was unable to fly through Hong Kong because of the pandemic, and so I went to Bali alone. This was the last time I was able to respond to the land that called me. I had some deep experiences with the land there, especially an ancient tree that spoke very powerfully to me. That journey was a completion of so many things, while also opening a doorway to a new chapter.

I've been home in Byron Bay ever since. My gypsy spirit has been dormant with the closing of our borders. I've felt frustration, boredom, anger and deep sadness. But I've also been drawn more deeply into the earth beneath me here in Byron Bay.

And just as Mark and I have had to reconcile to a virtual relationship, for now, I've had a similar reconciliation with the lands that call me from around the globe.

I know my work with the sacred portals around the earth isn't complete. But I now realise that I don't need to be there physically to access their energy. In my energetic work, I can bring through the power of a place, not only for myself but for my clients. We can all experience the energetic exchange with the earth that once required our presence but now simply requires our focus.

My work is evolving. I adore working with female entrepreneurs and the energy of their business, but I'm sensing a new facet to my work.

The earth's voice is getting louder as she experiences her evolution. She reminds me that my mission has always been about my connection to her and the songlines. I now see their flow linked to the energy of silver, a yin energy that opens us to receiving the earth's abundance in a way that we have never experienced before. I sense that my role is to activate the opening of this receiving channel in humanity as we move into the Aquarian age.

This vision is still not fully clear, but I have a deep knowing that it is my next chapter. From 2022 this wisdom will reveal itself with more clarity as I step into my new role as The Silver Seer. As always, I will wait for the earth to call and my heart will respond. This is the new way. This is the only way.

ABOUT THE AUTHOR

Jacquelyn Atkins supports female entrepreneurs to energetically connect to their businesses so they can easily attract their ideal clients.

A lifelong healer, her career shifted from physiotherapy to energy healing twenty years ago. As a sound healer, she facilitated retreats, taught workshops, and led journeys to sacred earth sites in France and Australia.

Moving online in 2017, Jacquelyn uses her clairvoyance and clairaudience to establish a co-creative relationship between her clients and their businesses. She removes the energetic blocks that hold them back from fully stepping into the personal and business success they desire.

Jacquelyn is passionate about supporting women from all over the world to discover and communicate their true message through their businesses. She is excited to embrace the next chapter of her business journey connecting her clients more powerfully with the abundant earth energies through the receptive power of silver.

Website: www.jacquelynatkins.com
Podcast: www.pod.link/bizalchemy
Insight Timer: www.insig.ht/jacquelyn
Email: email@jacquelynatkins.com

7

MARY GOODEN

I AM FREE

What are you waiting for?

These words echoed in my head for years before I decided to surrender. You are not the same as everyone else; you have a mission, a purpose and a destiny far beyond the human experience.

I have only ever imagined that I could be Free! Safe, supported and loved for the duration of this lifetime, in alignment with these vibrations on a cellular level.

Are you willing to stand in the reality that you are Free?

As a child, I felt trapped in an unrecognizable agenda. Tuning out was the only way in! Rules and regulations are meant to hold us back from our sovereignty, to keep us small and lifeless. I only ever wanted to be me. I was an empath, for sure. An empowered empath is the way I refer to it. I felt so much for others, but never to my own demise. The way I remember it, I was always coaching my peers on ways to release from their own misery. The energy that supported me was useful to so many, as people would constantly weave in and out of my life. I used my voice as a tool in all the ways imaginable, good, bad or indifferent. I believe that communication and courage are vehicles for powerful transformation. I had three very different siblings, and I mastered being the youngest, with a hefty opinion and a loud presence. Not a single one of us tried to be like the other, and our guide "mother" ignited the fire.

The mission to "breakthrough" to the very best version of you is a daunting and courageous task, not to be taken lightly. Those who refuse and resist their calling feel trapped by their own discouragement and disappointment. The human teachings have been designed to keep us hidden away in confusion, the assignment of never being satisfied and always wanting more.

I chose a great parental guide (mother). She set a beautiful example for my old soul yearnings. Her love was powerful, and her energy radiated creativity and freedom. She displayed a genuine work ethic of devotion and dedication. I seemed to mimic this immediately when I started my first real job. I was an asset to any position I sought. My insatiable desire to do what I wanted led me through some knowledgeable and partially dangerous experiences. Thank goodness I have a team of Guides and Angels with massive support and a sense of humor. I didn't always judge things as right or wrong; I went after life for the lesson, the experience, the gift!

High school is a joke, now more than ever. A class of constant comparison and judgment. It may only serve to keep the pharmaceutical companies at the top of the food chain and intertwined with political puppets. I spent years fighting this force-fed bullshit, as I reminded myself daily to live authentically and based on my own experience. This has been the path to my greatest expansion.

I graduated and left home when I was seventeen, ready to shine my light. I surely hit the ground running and eloped with a signed and notarized letter from my mother. I felt fully the permission to do whatever the fuck I wanted. I wasn't pregnant or worthless. I felt safe supported and loved every step of the way. I don't come with a load of childhood trauma or a grand list of karmic crap that may or may not show up. My shadow work is minimized, because I stopped hiding from myself early on. I stand in my beliefs, those that make my heart sing. I am almost positive that they differ from yours, because our mission is not the same. One of our greatest gifts in this lifetime is the permission to choose! Yes, that's right—each and every one of us have the power to choose our reality.

As a young adult, I was on fire! I married my first husband at age seventeen on a quest for the ultimate feeling of happiness and satisfaction. We spent twenty-two years building a massive kingdom, completely aligned with the societal version of success. I was motivated by titles, stature and money. I had the bull by the horns; I was in control; I was powerful, fearless, and oh so fortunate. I thought I was living my best life. I was a top-notch people pleaser. I was devoted to doing whatever made me look and feel accomplished. My success was defined by what I had, what I did, and how much money was in my bank account. I had to master being enough, knowing enough, and having enough.

Where are my meaningful life experiences? Where is my gratitude? Where is this going, and how do I feel about it? The song clamored in my head, "I can't get no satisfaction" oh, and I really felt like I was trying.

As a mother, I was invited to see, feel, and know the light. The first of my two angels came to life when I was twenty-seven. Emily was every bit of love, compassion and grace that was missing in my life. She was the catalyst of change that was desperately needed in my life. Her presence allowed me to pause and create a new dream for our family. Several years later, with great surprise, my wholehearted leader Kristen arrived on the scene. Her fiery passion filled every room. These two beautiful beings of light choose me to be their guide into the new world, and I wasn't going to let them down. They are every bit of the authentic, free-thinkers and conscious leaders that came here to create lasting change in the world!

Of course, this fairytale came with circumstances and experiences that offered growth and expansion for all of us. We survived disagreements, divorce and custody battles with minimal scars and a deep reverence for unconditional love.

I am "All In!" In the moment that felt like I was in the lowest vibration of my human experience, I uttered these words. I stood up and walked away from my final "pity party" and decided that it was time to surrender and celebrate. The twenty-five years that I lived loving the same man and creating two amazing daughters (Angels) was a Gift!

I am open to receive my Gifts!

I immediately surrendered to a daily practice of connecting with myself, my God and nature. I prayed for support, guidance and grace. If you are willing to ask for anything, be open and committed to receiving everything.

In a single moment, your whole life can change if you choose to allow it!

I chose to anchor into my five realities of Freedom!

Love - Only love is real. When we are aligned with the frequency of love, we are co-creating with our God, Divine, Source. Simply put, we are choosing Faith over Fear. Are you willing to see, be and share love, compassion and grace in all things?

Truth - Align with your most authentic self. Speak your truth from the heart. Discomfort exists in the confines of comparison, competition, guilt and shame that are societally impressed upon you. We are all beautiful, bright and brilliant. Are you committed to becoming the very best version of YOU?

Surrender - Liberate yourself from pain. Allow yourself to align with the magic and miracles that surround you. Surrender is about letting in the inspiration that wants to be birthed through you. Every experience is a gift. Are you open to receive your gifts?

Release - Radically let go of the bullshit! Choose to take off the mask, to stop playing small, to walk away from anything that isn't creating joy, peace and comfort in your life. Are you willing to be surprised in the uncertainty and successful in the synchronicity?

Remember - Effortlessly evolve on purpose. This is where the mission begins, where the ultimate glory is seen, felt and known. Every wish, desire and intention become your reality. Are you ready to choose your Divine Destiny?

We came here for such a time as this, to know freedom!

Are you ready to make your OWN choices, to get out of the societal box and reveal your gifts and your greatness?

The time is now!

Life gets better when you allow it, invite it, and embrace it. Open yourself again and again to the wonder, and do your part to live your most authentic life.

In the last eight years of my existence, I have been shown how every experience along my path has taught me to be more of me. I have felt the purest essence of gratitude and grace. I have been put on a platform for the world to see, for my children to embrace and for my soul family to acknowledge. I rise in God's honor daily and ask to be shown the way today. Every day I surrender to what is, not what has been or will be. My measure is not how much I have gained, but how many I have served. The resources and opportunities that have shown up in my life are beyond any dream that I have ever imagined. It is of no concern to me, what will happen tomorrow. Instead, how can I be all of me today? Who shall I serve and how shall I serve them? That is my wake-up call. I will not do this any other way and I am quickly realizing my teenage daughters will not either. God has gifted me a global gateway to share the voices an inspiration of others who have chosen the journey of their soul's mission. With daily surrender and divine guidance I have created beautiful containers for my dreams, which attract all the best support, relationships and opportunities. I am here to create loving and lasting change in the world.

I am free!

ABOUT THE AUTHOR

Mary Gooden is CEO and founder of Divine Destiny Publishing and Yoga Etc. She believes that abundance thrives in your ability to remain aligned and authentic, which is a daily practice. Mary has studied and practiced Yoga, Meditation and Reiki Energy Harmonizing for almost twenty years. By taking an intuitive approach, she focuses on creating a space for clients to embody Soul-Mastery, a mentorship program that awakens you to your wholehearted mission. Mary supports conscious visionaries, leaders, coaches and entrepreneurs in becoming published authors by sharing their powerful messages, stories and missions on a global platform. She has contributed to two #1 International Bestselling books and has created an International Bestselling book titled *Aligned Leaders*. As a limitless source of God's Love and Light, her intention is to restore inner harmony, authenticity, and freedom to as many individuals as possible. Mary currently shares her time between Sedona, Arizona and New Orleans, Louisiana with her husband and loving daughters.

Website: *www.yogaetcboutte.com*
Email: *divinereikilove@yahoo.com*
Facebook: *www.facebook.com/mary.s.gooden*
and www.facebook.com/groups/divinedestinypublishingevents
and www.facebook.com/groups/1269124473534757
Instagram: *www.instagram.com/mjgooden76*

8

SHAWNA SMITH

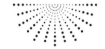

SEEDS ARE SOWN

I love understanding where we've come from. I believe you need to understand your roots to grow into an impressive tree. In the scriptures, you can study Heavenly Mother through references to trees. This symbolism is powerful both in spiritual study and earthly examples.

Roots are called the nervous system of the forest. Trees can connect their roots with others and share nutrients. It's truly a beautiful phenomenon and one to explore if you haven't heard of it.

Considering that the feminine divine is connected to tree symbolism, this alone can teach us so much about our role as women in the world. A tree growing in a forest builds the best homes because the trunk grows tall and straight. It makes better boards for shelters, without gaps that let in the cold. A large tree growing by itself on top of a hill may look impressive, but on close examination, its wood is gnarled and warped from supporting itself along the way.

What if we truly embraced the innate power we have to connect?

In stressful situations, a woman's brain immediately signals the desire to find someone to talk to, someone to help—in other words: connection. A man's brain goes into either immediate action (fight) or escape and avoidance (flight).

This is such a beautiful balance! As women, we are programmed to need and nourish each other. We build a beautiful and healthy forest by staying connected.

Ask for help. Find your forest. They are waiting to support and nourish you.

Now that we know how we are biologically programmed, let's discuss how the modern woman came into being.

Almost a thousand years ago, the western world proliferated the idea that women were cursed with childbirth. Prior to this, we had volumes of study of pregnancy in Greece with little to no reference to pain in childbirth except due to an extreme complication, in which case, herbs and tinctures were recommended.

Also during this time, women were tortured, killed, and forced into renouncing their healing gifts and knowledge. They were sent into isolation during childbirth to bear it alone, and any woman trying to help was convicted of heresy. There was an immediate spike in fear during childbirth that perseveres today. In cultures that were not exposed to this way of thinking, they still use birthing circles where women gather around the mother and hum and sway with her during contractions. They sing and dance the baby out together.

Using our root example from above, does your heart not sing at the idea of feeling only love, connection, support, and nourishment during childbirth?

Then, just about a hundred years ago, marketing began to take on a more modern edge. People realized you could create markets by convincing people they needed what you were selling—diamonds, cars, telephones, electricity. The marketing of things that are now everyday items had to be carefully crafted for people to want to change their lifestyle and make purchases that set them apart while still fitting into the rest of the neighborhood.

The personal safety razor came out in 1901, and sales shot through the roof. To increase markets and interest even more, they hopped on the coattails of rising hemlines and sleeveless dresses and convinced women they didn't want to look like undesirable monkeys. My mom still remembers the advertisements telling women they didn't want to be Neanderthals. Now we have an $18 billion industry built on the back of degrading and vilifying the natural state of a woman's body.

Whether or not you like shaving your legs, can we just take a moment to gaze forward from that point at the impact this has today on little girls' self-perception?

After a visit with family, my daughter brought up the concept of shaving legs because her cousin had just begun doing so. Unprompted, she said, "I don't want to shave my legs."

You don't have to, sweetie. You never have to do anything with your body that you don't want to do. And there is nothing wrong with any part of your body.

The world may tell you differently because we are highly motivated by fear. Fear of not fitting in. Fear of not being connected. Fear of being alone. On a hill. Wrestling for each inch of our life. By ourselves.

But we are also motivated by Love. And Love is more powerful than fear. Love for our body. Love for each other. Love for the strong roots, delicious soil, and cleansing rain. Love for all the women that came before us and all they were told and believed. Love for their pain that we can learn from and make things better. Love for their suffering that we can use to change the world. Love for ourselves in this moment right now, because that *is* the change in the world.

Place your hand on your heart for a moment and just feel that ancient love flowing through your veins. Feel how it connects you to all the good in the world.

You are the change.

MIRACLES HAPPEN EVERY DAY

"Every day we are engaged in a miracle which we don't even recognize"
- Thich Nhat Hanh

Five years ago, my estranged aunt reconnected with our family. It had been sixteen years of her solitude on the hill. I had always thought of her, always longed for a connection with her. I remember the phone call with my mom when she told me Kristy reached out and the excitement that jump-started a battery I didn't even know I had inside of me.

We began corresponding through letters and the occasional email. Her health worsened, and her situation became more dire. Together, my mom, Kristy, and I participated in a three-day fast to know and understand what the best next action would be.

From the very beginning, I knew I was meant to care for Kristy. I had no idea how I was going to make that work halfway across the country, with three small children, my marriage, and multiple businesses. But I knew this was the moment I had waited for my whole life.

In school, I used to doodle pictures of makeovers. I would draw a face and then add crazy hair, pimples, and other known to be less desirable attributes. Then I would draw the same features but makeover their hair, makeup, and clothes.

Makeovers are my thing. I love the before and after pictures of home remodels, body transformations, and home organization.

On a deeper level, I knew I was built to transform people's lives. I just didn't know my superpower yet. What was I really capable of?

So we fasted for three days. My mom got no answer. Kristy's only answer was one word: Shawna. And I had known the answer all along. Kristy needed to move to be near me.

At the time, we were living in Texas, and she was housebound in Montana, suffering from morbid obesity, a tracheostomy, congestive heart failure, restless leg syndrome, and a mysterious pain that wracked her whole body like one giant charley horse.

Needless to say, the "how" was escaping me. How could we move her partway across the country safely?

We were also getting ready to move two hours north, which felt slightly closer. We found a beautiful home on a couple acres with plenty of space to build a guest house if we wanted. And we also found the perfect home for Kristy, equipped with a sunroom, something she had loved about her former house and was quite difficult to find. The day before we put an offer on our house, we got a phone call. How about North Carolina?

My husband and I knew immediately that we were needed in North

Carolina. We changed all plans from moving North and poured every-thing into the move further East. Further from our parents and further from Kristy.

Within four months, we found a home, moved across the country with the help of my parents, and settled into a life of David working in Texas for six more months and visiting us on weekends whenever possible. I and our now four little children settled into our new home.

This fourth little one was a girl that came with a very special message. She was here to help Kristy. It kept me driving forward on the whole idea. I had to get these two spirits together.

Within two months of our move to North Carolina, I had the great fortune to meet and help a wonderful lady struggling with chronic pain and illness. She was in such a position that she had to sell her beautiful garden home. When I first began helping her, I wasn't even thinking about a home for Kristy yet. We had just unpacked, and I knew the right place would pop up at the right time.

About six weeks after meeting this lady, I received a very strong and clear message while washing dishes. You should buy this home for Kristy.

My husband and I considered it together, and he agreed right away. It was time to make plans for her move!

Knowing the only way possible to move her safely was an absolute miracle, I began praying for miracles. I studied them in scriptures and stories. I learned everything I could about miracles. Nine months after our move, we collected Kristy from Montana. And it truly was a journey of rebirth.

Our plan A was to fly her to North Carolina, with checked suitcases full of her primary needs, and send her other things in a moving truck. Plan B was to make half the plane ride and after missing the forty-five-minute connection, stop overnight somewhere with a hospital bed and restructure a second flight. Plan C was she couldn't make it on the first plane, and we rented some kind of accessible RV to drive her across the country.

My parents made several trips to help sort through her storage unit and apartment and pre-organize as much as possible. I flew out with my dad for three whirlwind days of final packing and loading up a moving truck. We had so much support from her caregivers and our church members in the area. Everything they took care of before I arrived and cleaned up after we left was truly a blessing. Miracle number one.

At the time, I was two months pregnant with my fifth child. Using my knowledge from previous pregnancies about the spiritual nature of pregnancy and birth, I could stay conscious of nourishing my body and baby while working around the clock to sort through piles of papers, boxes of medical supplies, and other household items to bring everything she needed. So I still felt great and energized during a time it's usually best to rest and reflect. Miracle number two.

A few months before helping Kristy, I flew on a plane that was the same model we booked for her flight. We bought her two first-class seat tickets at the front so she wouldn't have to walk down the aisle and would fit in the seats with plenty of room. I hadn't flown in a long time as we typically drove across the country. To this day, I cannot honestly remember why I made the flight. But as I walked onto the plane, I noticed the first-class seats had a problem. The armrests didn't lift. The seats were slightly wider, but the armrests didn't come up. There was no way for Kristy to fit into just one seat. I called the airline and discussed the problem; they acknowledged that should've been mentioned by the teller when we purchased the tickets and allowed us a refund and helped us change the tickets. Miracle number three.

While we were packing, I needed three extra-large suitcases. She lived in the town of Missoula, which is a little smaller and there weren't a lot of retail options. Also, we were packing on a budget, so I couldn't just go buy brand new ones. I prayed and visualized what I needed and went to the local Goodwill store. I found exactly what I was looking for. And if you know me and my history of consignment shopping, this was truly the biggest miracle of them all!

The morning of the move arrived, and we made it into the Medical Transport van on time. Miracle number four.

We arrived early at the airport with nine carry-on bags and our three large suitcases. As we walked up to the customer service desk, their faces drained of all color, and they politely stammered we wouldn't be able to take all that on the plane. I quickly explained to them we had arrived three hours early so they could help us repack the right way. With immense relief, the poor attendant explained exactly what our journey would look like and which carry-on bags were best and which had to be merged and packed away.

I went to work with my lifetime experience and inherited super packing skills and got everything down to just two carry-on bags. Miracle number five. We made it up to our gate with time for a snack and final farewells with her primary caregiver and dear friend, Micky.

The plane arrived early. Miracle number six and one I prayed seriously hard for. It took us forty-five minutes to make it to row number nine, the first row available with armrests that moved where we could also store her medical equipment at her feet. Because of her weight, they couldn't use the aisle chair to wheel her to her seat. She had to walk from the front of the plane the whole way to the ninth row. Miracle number seven.

Even with our time delay, the last person boarded the plane just in time for an on-schedule take-off. Miracle number eight.

An overhead bin wouldn't latch, and we couldn't take off until a maintenance man came. We didn't know it at the time, but this delay would be one of our biggest miracles.

The people around us maintained a very positive attitude, or at least we felt like they were positive. Miracle number nine.

After landing in Dallas for our connection (there was no possibility of a direct flight from Missoula to North Carolina), we waited patiently for the plane to de-board and then Kristy, now stiff and sore from sitting and her previous walk made her way off the plane. It took us an hour. It was the plane's last stop of the day and they didn't need to re-board. Miracle number ten.

At the airplane door, a beautifully composed woman apologized that the delayed flight caused us to miss our next flight. She had a list of other flights we could catch that were coming up. If someone could pick us up in Raleigh, we could board the plane right away and get to North Carolina tonight! Miracle number eleven.

When we bought our house in Greensboro, we moved in next door to the most amazing neighbors you could ever ask for. Our neighbor, aptly named Joy, and her wheelchair-bound husband, Adam, had a wheelchair accessible van. I knew without even having to ask that she would be happy to allow us to use the van to pick up my aunt. So I said yes to the new flight plan and called my mom and Joy as we rushed to the next gate to make sure everyone was okay with the new plan. In addition, they said this plane was a little bigger and would be more comfortable for my aunt. Miracle numbers twelve and thirteen.

With help, we made it to the gate, and I excitedly stepped onto the plane. They were able to give us row ten so we would be as close to the front as possible. But as I stepped up the aisle, it seemed to stretch on for eternity. My heart sank all the way to my feet and tears almost sprang out of my eyes. Without reserve, I whispered, "they said this plane would be bigger." The sweet flight attendant replied, "oh, it is, Honey!"

But the aisle was smaller.

To accommodate the bigger seat sizes, there was slightly less aisle space. Also, the entire plane was already boarded. We were the last ones. Every seat filled with expectant passengers watching. And it had just taken an hour to get off the plane from row nine.

I looked to my right where a labored, red-faced, exhausted, but eternally positive Kristy was shifting from her wheelchair to make the walk to the aisle. I smiled, took a deep breath, and walked to our row to get everything ready for her to sit down. After prepping, I stood up in the aisle by our seat and said, "I would just like to thank you in advance for your patience." Immediately, several people responded with affirmations and asked if there was anything they could do to help. Miracle number fourteen. I said, "positive thoughts would be most welcome, thank you!"

It took her fifteen minutes to walk from the airplane door to the front of the aisle. A man in a seat in the front row asked, "Would you like to have my seat?" Miracle number fifteen. He quickly gathered his things and said, "where were you sitting?" I gathered up her things, and he made himself comfortable by the window.

These first-class seats were much wider and the aisle armrest folded up, so Kristy could fit in one seat. Miracle number sixteen. As she moved toward it, the woman in the seat by the window spoke up. "Um, am I going to be able to get off when we land?"

It was a valid question. Once Kristy was sitting, it would be very difficult to get past her and off the plane. The lady looked at me; I looked at the flight attendant; the flight attendant looked at both of us. And for a moment, the question just hung in the air. "Do you have a connecting flight?" I asked. "No, but I have a husband who is waiting for me," she replied.

From behind me, a small voice said, "She can have my seat and then you can both sit together." I turned around and this beautiful soul stood up out of her first-class seat, and without another word, moved back to row ten to join the other angel. Miracle number seventeen.

As we got settled, I went to plug Kristy's oxygen machine into the outlet on our seats. We had several long-life batteries but with her breathing efforts, we had gone through them much quicker than expected and the last battery was just about to die. "Perfect timing," I thought. But when I plugged the machine in, nothing happened. There wasn't enough electricity to power her oxygen machine at the seats.

Hopeful, I asked the flight attendant if there was an outlet around the corner that we could use. He took the cord and said, "I'll see what I can do." It made it by a hair! If she sat down in any other seat, we would not have been able to plug in her oxygen machine. Miracle number eighteen.

The entire journey was full of cheerful, gracious, helpful, and kind staff and passengers. I've never had a travel experience like that before or since. Miracle number nineteen.

Kristy made it home safely into her own bed and her new garden home. We nurtured her body back to a measure of health, and eventually, she was able to triple her distance walked, lose ninety-eight pounds, and regain daily activities like showering, prepping food, trimming rose bushes, and sewing. She passed away seven months later in such a state of deep, soulful peace. Five days before she passed away, she asked my mom, "Why would God care about me?"

And my mom shared this story.

"Well, Kristy, you like puzzles. Imagine you are finished with the puzzle and one piece is missing. How important is that piece now?"

With that knowledge, she surrendered to a world where love waited for her.

You are the final puzzle piece, and we need you. You matter. You make a difference.

~

We each have a role to play. Who do you serve? What ignites your passion for life? Commit to it all in. Nothing can stop you. We are our only obstacle.

Through helping Kristy, I healed my roots and assembled all the puzzle pieces of my life and business. From the family activity center we both dreamed of separately to the opportunity to guide someone willingly through a complete healing journey. The full picture came together. I heal, I teach, I grant wishes. I do it all.

The core of my body vibrated for hours after I realized my truest calling. Like the string of my life was plucked by recognition: "I am teaching Abundance in Motherhood."

You can be a mom, an empress, a wife, and yourself! You don't have to pick and choose, you don't have to compartmentalize. I can work with my baby on my lap running an empire. My uniform has yogurt smeared on my shoulder and boogers wiped on my pants.

And I still show up, because the message is important. Not the volume in my hair or the length of my eyelashes. You can't stop the message. The Dream. The Dream that moms make a difference in their beautiful, regularity of daily life. That they know they hold the key to their own dream. That they have the power all along to step out of the prison of their body, expectations, anxieties, and self-judgements and into freedom.

You have an abundance of time. You have an abundance of energy. You have an abundance of support. You have an abundance of love. You live a life of Abundant Motherhood.

The world doesn't need someone trying to be like everyone else. It needs you. Being you. Just you.

ABOUT THE AUTHOR

Shawna Smith is a visionary and a mom of five. She is a women's health advocate and educator. She helps busy women find relief from menstrual pain and to love living in their bodies through every phase of life. She loves animals of all kinds, movie marathons, and pictures of the beach... but not necessarily being at the beach. She is passionate about creating a world where women can trust their intuition about their individual health journey.

Website: www.health-and-harmony.passion.io
and www.spiritualchildbirth.com
Facebook: www.facebook.com/groups/tiredmomsisterhood

9

ABIGAIL MENSAH-BONSU

"When I let go of who I am, I become who I might be."
- Lao Tzu

Hello, beautiful light,
I invite you to take a sacred journey with me.
A journey of freedom, transformation, evolution, and reclamation of the sacred self.

Before we begin, let's get energetically centered and consciously call in our divine support and guidance.

Begin by breathing into your heart.

Imagine a golden ball of Christ consciousness light at the top of your head. Open up and ask the ball of light to come into your heart and anchor within.

Now, bring your awareness to your roots, sending them deep into the earth. There, at the center of the earth, imagine a fifth-dimensional crystalline ball of light representing the divine mother's heart matrix, and just like you did above, open up and bring that ball of light into your heart.

Breathe and experience this merging within your heart. Now, call in the presence and frequency of your higher self to come into your heart.

With your breath, see all three lights merge into one starlight, bright, overflowing, and magnetic, expanding through you and all around you.

Then read aloud or decree clearly in your mind:

I now call upon divine light, my higher self, the presence, and frequency of my very own divine team of guides, guardians, angels, archangels, ascended Masters of the highest and the most benevolent light.

I call upon the love, support, and guidance that is here for me. I ask that you support me in becoming clear and open to receive the guidance, love, and frequency here now within these pages.

I ask to be surrounded, filled, and illuminated with divine white light.

Cleanse and purify my energy.

Uplift my vibration.

And support me in embodying my highest divine truth and potential.

May I hear what I need to hear, see what I need to see, know what I need to know, and receive all that is meant for my highest good and for the highest good of all.

May the light continue to align, activate and amplify within us all.

And so it is.

UNCENSORED. UNTAMED. UNLEASHED.

When I think about these three words, I am reminded of how my soul operates and what drives me.

I've always been one who paves her own way. You can say I was born that way thanks to my rebel, leader, and goddess archetypes who make sure that I am following my own path. My thinking is innovative and dynamic. I am highly intuitive, and with all my clairs activated, I see the world very differently from most. Where there is rigidity, rules, control, I am able to see and invite in a world of infinite possibilities.

I believe that as we move more and more into 2022 and beyond, people are craving to know themselves on a deeper level. We are all being asked to tap into something deeper within, to go beyond what we think we know. We are being called to embody more of our soul essence and to release all the learned programs and constructs within ourselves and our world that no longer serve us. We are being invited to come back home and to remember who we really are.

After going through the transformations of the last three years, many people are hearing the call to come within, reconnect with their soul and ask the sacred questions: Who Am I? What is My Purpose?

As I'm writing this chapter, I am in the process of changing. I feel myself shifting, evolving, and transforming into a new person. Every now and then, I go through this stage, which I call the Phoenix stage. Just when I think I have reached a certain point of balance and stability, the next level shows its head, where again I get to uplevel, integrate and embody that next level of my being. and I have reached that point again.

It's really not about the destination, is it? It's about the journey. It's about the path, the crystallization of the wisdom, that we receive as we walk on our path.

THE PHOENIX CHILD

I recently discovered this about myself: when presented with a challenge that is for my highest good, I will walk through the fire to get to the other side. It doesn't matter how hard or long it might take because I know what's on the other side is where I want to be. I am fearless when it comes to growth and expansion.

The Phoenix has been one of my power animals for a long time. She taught me that no matter how hard life gets, it won't last forever. No matter how far I fall, I can always get back up like the boss Goddess that I am. She taught me how to use the alchemical fires to burn away the karmic heaviness and anything in my way. She taught me not to be afraid of death and that death is part of the cycle of life. She taught me that every time an old part of me dies, which has happened many times in the past and is happening at present, a new me arises higher and more aligned than before. She showed me my wings and my freedom. I learned to release the heaviness so I could fly higher, discovering new heights of myself and my visions.

Early in October, I woke up with a strong desire to really connect deeply with myself. I found myself thinking about when was the last time that I felt like and truly saw myself. When was the last time I touched my scalp? When was the last time I saw the shape of my head? I had this deep desire to really get to know me. The idea of shaving my head popped into my mind. Now, there's a thought that's very foreign to me.

I've always loved long hair and always imagined myself having long flowy hair to my back. To think about cutting my hair is something I didn't see coming.

The more I looked at myself in the mirror, the more I couldn't recognize myself, and the more I craved to touch my soul. I wanted to look in the mirror and see my soul reflected back at me, to see who I really am. So I began to mention it to my husband who was tickled by the idea of seeing his wife with short hair for the first time.

Who am I without my hair?

When you have a deep soul longing, the synchronicities that begin to follow are quite out of this world. I began seeing videos of women who just shaved their heads for a purpose or to manifest something. There was an episode on the Red Table Talk show with Jada Smith where she and her daughter shaved their heads, and they were talking about how that felt, and what that did for them. As I listened, I was in tears because I felt it. I felt and knew this was what I needed to do.

And so one day, my husband went to work and I began to chop off my hair. I just grabbed the scissors, and I cut it short. When my husband got home, I gave him the shaver, and I sat down and said I'm ready. And while he was giggling, he shaved my head, and I can't even explain to you how I felt.

With each clump of hair that fell on my lap, I felt lighter and free. I was home. I looked at myself in the mirror afterward and smiled. I had the biggest genuine smile on my face ever. I said hello to myself and I smiled even more. I touched and massaged my scalp and it felt exhilarating.

I was home. Each morning I get up and go to the bathroom and see my reflection in the mirror, I stop and smile and I say hello. I don't remember the last time that I did that. I don't remember the last time that I looked at myself in the mirror and truly saw me. Even writing this brings me to tears.

Who would have thought that I would find home within myself by shaving my head?

There's so much fear associated with letting go. But just like nature, when it's time to let go, we are surrounded by beauty. Nature shows us the beauty of letting go and the vibrancy of life.

When you release, you make space for something new and beautiful to come through. When you do, release it back to the earth, so that it can be transmuted into new energy, which will circle back around and come to bless you. Don't be afraid to release that which is ready to go and that which no longer serves you.

Make space for the new and better to come through.

I had to release the very thing that I prized the most. This taught me that we get to a point in life where we've accumulated a lot of things through our experiences. And we reach a point where we need to shed everything and become naked. When we are naked, we can come back home to ourselves and truly see ourselves. Our true core self is hidden underneath all that rubble and clutter. It is in times like this when we feel the desire to dig deeper and shed. We need to release the old and outdated in order to find ourselves again.

What part of you is itching to be acknowledged at this time?

To be honest, I don't think I want to grow my hair back. I am loving it so much, just being able to touch and massage my scalp. Don't get me started on shower time. Having the water fall on my scalp is ecstatic and delightful. Each day, I love myself more and more and I feel my soul, which is all I've ever wanted.

I see who I really am.

I had to shed all the old hurt, pain, and trauma, the beliefs that no longer work, and the thought patterns that were holding me back. I let it all go. I transferred all of it into my hair and as my husband shaved it off, I felt a million times lighter. I saw my starlight shine brighter than ever, my soul came through.

One of my greatest virtues and core dreams is freedom. My soul desires to feel free in this life. My soul yearns to freely express itself, to feel light, to experience the best that life's got to offer. I don't want to be held down by the rules and regulations of life.

I want to be free.

I want my wings to be wide open and to fly whenever and wherever I want just like my spirit flies every day.

I yearn to be free. And so in everything that I do, if it feels heavy, tied down, and restricted, I know it is not my path. My true path feels light. It feels open, free, ecstatic, and juicy. It's uncharted. I get to create my own path as a wayshower and leader as I go.

I've been listening to a song by Fia called Nature of Love lately and can't get enough of it. It speaks of my current journey. The lyrics go:

"I empty myself over again
Nothing to be or to achieve
Simple beautiful clarity
I lay down my sword at your feet

Spirit move me
Where would you have me go
Spirit show me
What do I need to know
I surrender it all
Can't fight anymore
Take me in your arms
And teach me the nature of Love

I am reborn
My heart is open wide
Flowing with grace
Through time and space
Finally I feel my place
I lay down my sword at your feet

May the light of my soul
Keep guiding me home

Spirit move me
Where would you have me go
Spirit show me
What do I need to know
I surrender it all
Can't fight anymore
Take me in your arms
And teach me the nature of Love"

There is power in letting go. When we relinquish control over what we think we know, should be, or do, miracles happen. We find ourselves home again, remembering why we began this journey in the first place and what we are here to do. Society taught us to accumulate and spirit asks us to shed and release to find our true selves again.

I believe this cycle of receiving and releasing is a part of the human experience. As we journey through life, we fill our cups with the wisdom and golden nuggets from our many life experiences. We get to a point where the cup becomes full and there is no more room to receive.

We reach a crossroad where we can choose to either hold on until we get stuck, outdated, and stagnant or release the contents of the cup and make space for the new and improved level to show up.

As the old crumbles and dissolves, many find themselves in a place of fear and in the unknown. The old is gone. The new hasn't revealed itself yet and what is left is the now. Because society has taught us to always be either in the future or stuck in the past, most people don't know what to do when all that is left is the now. Yet the wisdom, the true gift is being present.

What you do in the now creates your future.

Every decision you make, every step you take, everything you say yes or no to is what creates your future. I hope that now you understand why the Now is so important and is such a vital place to operate in full awareness.

It's okay to feel fear, to be afraid in the state of the unknown. It's okay to be afraid of not knowing what is coming up next or not being able to see the complete picture of what is ahead of you.

YOUR HIGHER SELF AND DIVINE TEAM

We are not meant to walk this sacred journey by ourselves.

We came into this lifetime with thousands of spiritual supporters to help and guide us through this lifetime. One of the main things that I teach, is rebuilding the connection with your higher self and your divine team. It is life-changing.

When was the last time that you tuned in to your highest self or checked in with your divine team to see what step you can take today that fulfills you, brings you joy, or your dream life?

When was the last time you checked in with your divine team and asked them to go out there and bring to you all that you need to help you create your best life?

This is what they're here for. Whether you are aware of them or not, they are always here with you. One thing they cannot do is go against your free will. Which means that you have to ask for their assistance, support, and guidance.

It's a matter of awareness, beginning to tap into who you are at your highest self-expression which will bridge, create and strengthen that connection so you can begin to streamline higher consciousness from your higher self to you.

You have a whole team of angels, archangels, animal guides, masters of light, ancestors of the highest light who have signed up to work with you and are always with you, ready and eager to support and guide you.

I'm going to walk you through a soul exercise that will reconnect you to your higher self and your divine team. This is an exercise that you can do every morning, first thing when you wake up and the last thing when you go to sleep. It will help you strengthen that connection to the infinite possibilities, the infinite wisdom that is here for you.

Shall we begin!

SOUL PRACTICE

Bring your awareness back to your heart.

Call the presence of your higher self within your heart by saying:

I now invoke the presence, light, and consciousness of my higher self into my heart.

See, sense or feel your higher self emerge within your heart infusing her light and radiance into every part of your being.

Breath.

Imagine, sense, or feel a vibrant divine light that is all around you. As you breathe in, imagine you're drawing it into every cell of your being. Imagine every cell opening up to absorb this divine light. Breath the light into your mind, your heart, into your organs until your whole being begins to radiate.

Bring your awareness above your head. Visualize a golden ball of light above your head. Envision this ball of light begin to descend down through your crown and around you. And, as it does it, cleanses and clears your energy field, your mental body, your emotional body, your physical body, and your spiritual body.

Anything ready to be released gets pulled out. Any limiting beliefs, stagnant thought patterns, blockages, any dis-ease within the body and within the cells, release it to the golden ball of light. This higher consciousness is clearing you and setting you free at this time. Let it move all the way down, through the layers of the earth until it reaches the center of the Earth where it connects with the heart of the divine mother. There it surrenders.

Now bring your awareness back to the top of your head. Notice a beautiful crystalline diamond platinum pillar of light descending down, entering your crown, down through your body, and anchors into the Earth. Visualize this pillar of light expanding out all around you.

This pillar of light is filled with your I AM presence, your highest consciousness. And now open up your heart and begin to receive the light from above, from the heart of the divine father. Bring it down and anchor it within your heart. Open your heart to also receive the divine light and love from the divine mother below. Pull it up and anchor it within your heart. Allow those two lights to join together and expand into a beautiful crystalline bubble of light all around you. Breathe in this space of centeredness, wholeness, and connection.

And now repeat after me:

I now call upon my divine presence, I Am that I Am, my higher self, and my divine team of angels, archangels, ascended masters, animal guides, ancestors of the highest light who have signed up to work with me in this lifetime.

I ask that you lead the way, light up my path, and align me to my highest potential. Help me to fully show up in my divine radiance.

Help me to embody my divine light so I can be of greater service.

I ask that you bring me clear guidance as I navigate my sacred path.

Remove anything that blocks me from my Greatness, joy, radiance, and my livelihood. Take the lead, divine team, and show me my next step.

Bring to me miracles and blessings of infinite possibilities.

Bring to me all that I need to thrive and succeed in this life.

I thank you.

I love you.

And so it is.

I invite you to do this every day for twenty-one days and watch your path open up.

To me, being untamed is connected to the wild archetype within and that is the soul. The more we accept and honor our unique signature, we are able to express ourselves in a unique way and exactly what the world needs. We are able to share our own unique codes with society.

Uncensored is giving the heart permission to lead. It is the ability to speak from the heart, the center of our Multidimensional being, your true sacred voice. The true voice of your I Am presence which is undiluted, pure, and true to you.

When we are able to express our soul's unique signature and speak from the heart and true voice, we become unleashed and free.

There's no one true or right way of doing things or living your life. There's only your heart's way. Your soul has the map and blueprint that the heart follows. The sooner you operate from your heart, the clearer things will become and flow with ease. It doesn't mean there won't be any challenges. Rather, you will have access to the tools that will help you move through all the challenges that come your way.

Be bold.

Be courageous.

Have faith.

Trust that all is working out in your favor always.

Let go and Remember who you truly are.

I love you and I believe in you!

ABOUT THE AUTHOR

Abigail Mensah-Bonsu is the founder of the Moon Goddess Publishing and Moon Goddess Academy. She is an Elevated Consciousness and Divine Feminine Embodiment Mentor, Multidimensional Healer, three times #1 International Bestselling Author, and host of the Sovereign Divinity podcast.

Abigail works with Master souls, Leaders, Visionaries, Wayshowers, Lightworkers and Powerhouse women to bridge the gap between their physical and spiritual selves so they can maximize their success, creating greater impact, more money and an aligned resonant magical life.

She activates women into their Greatness, inspiring them to truly own their Divine Essence, Presence, Power, and Worth to create a high vibration life that is aligned with their divine birthright, creating their own version of Heaven on Earth. She lovingly and powerfully reminds her clients of what they really are beyond the limitations that they are currently perceiving, which is that they are powerful and limitless.

She helps her clients remember who they really are, breaking down the mental constructs, illusions and programmings and removing all those masks. Freedom is the result.

Website: www.moongoddessacademy.com
Facebook: www.facebook.com/groups/MoonGoddessSanctum
Instagram: www.instagram.com/intuitivegoddesscoach
Youtube: www.youtube.com/c/ABIGAILMensahBonsu
Podcast: www.anchor.fm/sovereigndivinity

ALICIA CRAMER

THINK BIG, RELEASE THE LIMITS, AND CREATE THE LIFE YOU WANT

T was sitting in my office, staring blankly at my computer, thinking to myself, "shouldn't I be happier?" I had just had one of the most profitable months in my business, and as much as I was feeling appreciation for my success, I was also feeling disappointed... and angry with myself. I still was not where I knew I could be.

Isn't it interesting how the mind works? For years, I helped my clients achieve exceptional success in their businesses and personal lives, convincing myself that I was content with my mediocre success. And it was when I finally broke through to a new income bracket that I took a difficult and honest look at myself and admitted that here I was... holding myself back. Oh, the feeling of hypocrisy. The way we justify our self-inflicted limitations. The very thing I was lovingly pushing my clients through, I was ignoring in my own life. I was still playing small, and my results showed it.

I strongly believe there are way too many amazing individuals called to do big, wonderful things in life, and their business is their vehicle to do those things. But they are held back by their old, limited subconscious conditioning. And because of those seemingly justifiable limitations, they live a life that is not nearly as fulfilling as it could be. So many entrepreneurs play small, as though that is the safer bet, yet knowing, on some deeper level, that it is not.

This chapter is for people who are ready to break free from their own self-imposed limitations. Those who are feeling the call to be and do and have more in life. Those who understand that they only get one opportunity to live this life and that they are not willing to get to the end of it full of regrets. So, if that is you, I am truly grateful to have this moment of your attention... to tell you, you CAN have the life you want... and to provide you with a seemingly simple technique to help break through resistance on your way to creating it.

First, I want to highlight the broader reason you may not be where you want to be in life and business, and even more importantly, how you can radically accelerate your results from this moment forward.

Regardless of what you have experienced in your life up to this very minute, even if it has been riddled with trauma and negativity, you can create a future that is richly fulfilling, abundant, and congruent with what you genuinely want. I know because I've been there, and so have many of my clients; and on some level of your being, you know it to be true for you... but if you are honest with yourself, you may not fully believe it. Why?

We know that we are conditioned (filled with conflicting and, many times, disempowering beliefs) throughout our lives. How many times have you heard, read, or witnessed things that promoted fear, scarcity, lack and limitation? A lot. So, of course, there is stuff in your subconscious mind that does not support your success. We will get to how to deal with that stuff shortly. Right now, though, I want you to consider how many times you've dreamed big? Really honestly looked at your true heart's desires. Aside from the occasional wishful thinking, how much of your time have you spent setting big goals and achieving them? Probably not nearly as much time as you have spent feeling disempowered, fearful, disappointed, and playing it safe.

You simply cannot recondition your mind to support you in creating the life you truly want with your old, limited thinking. You must do things differently.

90

I want to challenge you, right now, to stop for a moment, and as if your very life depends on it, dream bigger than ever before.

What do you really want?

If you knew you could not fail, what would you do?

If you knew you could figure out anything that you set your mind to, what would you choose to create?

Why do you want these things, and who will it positively impact besides yourself?

(Stop and think about this.)

I sincerely hope you took some time to contemplate these questions. If you did, you likely noticed a couple different things. On one hand, it felt good when you connected with those desires, and on the other, you encountered some resistance and doubt. Resistance and doubt are natural as you are up-leveling. Your mind doesn't have a frame of reference for some of these new ways of being, doing, and having. Rather than allowing those negative feelings to stop you, I want to briefly address a powerful strategy for creating new subconscious conditioning that will cause your mind to work with you—for the accomplishment of your big goals—instead of against you, as it has in the past.

See, if you look at the results you've gotten up to this point, it matches your expectations (aka beliefs). You will not deviate far from your current expectations. However, as you fill your mind with thoughts, feeling, images, and the energy of what you want, you begin to create empowering new subconscious programs, and effectively condition your mind to believe that it is in fact possible for you.

Tools like vision boards, visualization techniques, and various other practices can help reinforce your belief building. Also, physically being surrounded by and touching the material things you want helps create new patterns in the subconscious mind that support your belief that it is possible for you to have them. The more frequently you see, hear, and feel what you want, the higher your level of belief... and your beliefs become your reality. That is why many successful people say their circumstances in life changed when they started to spend time with people who already had wealth, success, or whatever they were aspiring to create. When you spend time around people who have already achieved those higher-level results, the mind is influenced to think, feel, and believe bigger than before, and you create new expectations for yourself.

Those behaviors help get positive momentum flowing toward achieving what you want in life. As you move toward your goals, you will encounter the subconscious programs that do not serve you in achieving your desired outcome. That includes the fears, doubts, insecurities, and limiting beliefs from your old subconscious conditioning. So, let's now take some time to talk about what to do when you bump up against that resistance.

To this point, you have already overcome an abundance of mental conditioning to get to where you are. Yet you know you could be doing better. You could have more money, more happiness, and more fulfillment. To get to the next level, and every up-leveling after that, you must continue to challenge your old fears, doubts, and insecurities. Those old patterns are always masked by seemingly justifiable excuses. It will require self-honesty to call yourself out and evaluate your old stories of limitation. This is an ongoing process.

Experiencing negative emotions is an indicator that one of those old mental programs has been triggered. Instead of trying to push it away, ignore it, or positive talk yourself out of it; give yourself permission to look at it. If you don't properly release it, it will persist in your subconscious mind and hold you back as it has so effectively done in the past.

From this point forward, when you notice a negative emotion that seems to interfere with your success, ask yourself, "what am I afraid of here?" If you are committed to seeing what is really going on in your mind, you will become aware of the old belief. It may simply appear to be a memory, but notice there is a fear or belief attached to it. Regardless of what you identify, ask yourself, "is it serving me to hold on to this?" Since no negative pattern is truly serving you, the answer to that question should be 'no'.

If, for some reason, your mind wants to justify why you should hold on to it, challenge that further. For instance, if you believe that holding on to a fear of putting yourself out there with your message is dangerous, dig deeper. Is it truly dangerous? Does it have to be? Is there a law of the Universe that says it must be so?

As you use discernment to challenge your old beliefs, the absurdity of holding on to them surfaces. Ask yourself again, "Is this serving me?" When the answer is 'no', ask yourself the next question: "Is this serving anyone at all?" Since your being fearful or disempowered is of no value to anyone, the answer will be 'no'. If it is not, challenge those beliefs just as you did with the first question, until the authentic answer within you is 'no'.

The final question to ask yourself is, "am I willing to let this go?" If you have gone through the process correctly, the answer to this question will be 'yes'. You should feel a willingness to release the fear, past hurt, or negative pattern. This simple decision, when done as stated, will allow you to let it go. It may not feel like an otherworldly shift. That is okay. Assuming you went through the process and genuinely saw with discernment that the old fear or belief is not serving you or anyone and you are willing to let it go, most of the time you will effectively release it without having to dig deeper into your issue.

When you make this a regular practice in your day-to-day life, it can help you rapidly release old limitations. Do not allow your mind to discredit this process because of its simplicity; it is powerful.

Society has trained us to believe that complexity means better. Yet, there is an abundance of evidence to the contrary. Now, I am not saying that all complexity is unnecessary or unbeneficial. What I am saying is that there are many things in life that we overcomplicate. Our inner struggles are often overcomplicated. When we understand how the mind works, we can unravel the overwhelming sense of disempowerment and take our inner power back.

When I started my hypnotherapy practice over a decade ago, clients would frequently come to me, hoping that hypnosis would magically solve their long-term struggle. After all, a technique shrouded in conspiracy and mystic might just be the only cure to their relentless issue. I would lovingly explain that no single technique is the cure-all per se, that nearly any technique can help them achieve their goal if and when they are truly committed to changing their behavior and/or life. The distinction between whether or not any technique works is based on two primary factors. 1) You are genuinely committed to achieving your desired outcome. 2) You believe that the method to create the desired outcome will work for you.

Let me distill that down even further to two important words: 'commitment' and 'belief'.

With hypnotherapy (and even now as a mindset coach and mentor), I had to help move my clients into commitment before the technique could really help them. And the process of hypnosis was really just the stage show to boost their belief that the technique would, in fact, help them. You already have the power to shift your beliefs, and it literally only takes a few moments when the commitment is there, and the old patterns have been challenged and/or replaced.

Now that I have explained what to do when you encounter negative emotions that indicate you've triggered an old self-limiting pattern, you must commit to the process to release it. Like everything in life, practice and repetition will create mastery, and after a while, it will be easier and faster to identify and release the very things that have held you back from the life you desire.

To recap the process:

- Be aware that the negative emotion you are experiencing is indicating you've triggered a disempowering belief or pattern.
- Take a moment to identify what has been triggered. It is often a fear, doubt, or insecurity. Sometimes, that takes the form of an old hurt from an experience that hasn't been properly released.
- Ask yourself, "is it serving me/helping me to hold on to this emotion/pattern/fear?"
- If 'no,' move on to the next question. If 'yes', dig deeper and find out why your mind believes it is helping you by holding on to the fear or resentment, etc. Then challenge whether it is, in fact, helping you or if there is a better way to feel moving forward. (Remember: There is always a better way than holding on to negative emotions.) Once you've challenged all your old reasons for holding on, you'll get to a 'no' response to the question. Then you can move on.

- Now, ask yourself, "is it serving anyone at all for me to hold on to this?"
- If 'no,' move on to the next question. If 'yes', dig deeper again until you've challenged all your old reasons for holding on. Once you get to a 'no' response, you can move on.
- Finally, ask yourself, "am I willing to let this go?"
- At this point, you should feel a slight shift emotionally. The triggered emotion you felt before on this issue should be gone. If more negative emotions come up, look to see if there is another old belief or pattern that is triggered and repeat the process.

Let me leave you with a couple of considerations. I've been doing my inner work for a very long time. It is the only reason I could overcome a painful childhood, major depression throughout my teens into my early adult life, trauma from an assault in my mid-twenties, and crushing financial setbacks in my early business ventures. It is the only reason for the success that I have created. The inner work is essential; however, there is an important element to inner work that many well-meaning people do not understand, which creates huge setbacks. Let's address that so you can avoid it.

As you start experiencing positive shifts from using various techniques, it is tempting to fixate on fixing everything you don't like about yourself or anything you perceive to be a potential issue in your life. But the more you focus on finding things to fix, the more things you will find to fix, and before you know it, you are off your positive momentum track and feeling disempowered and overwhelmed.

The solution is to make your goals and the positive aspects of your life the primary focus. Remember what you truly desire. Stay predominantly focused on what you are intentionally creating. Learn from your mentors, keep taking action toward your goals, and enjoy life. As you are on your right track, you will occasionally bump up against those old fears, doubts, and insecurities. When you do, that is when you use this or other techniques to shift them. After you've done your inner work to release the negative emotions, get right back to focusing on your goals.

95

I hope that you are committed to doing the big, wonderful things you are being called to do. Maybe, like me, you waited far longer than you needed to start playing a bigger game. But, like me, you are filled with unlimited, untapped potential. Awareness that you are the only one holding you back takes courage and is just the beginning. As soon as you decide to do what is necessary to create a life you won't regret, all the inspiration, mentors, and resources you need to support you on your journey will show up at exactly the right time. Keep saying 'yes' to yourself, even when you bump up against your old self-limiting beliefs... when you do, challenge them, release them... and get right back on track. You got this!

ABOUT THE AUTHOR

Alicia Cramer is an internationally recognized Business Mindset Expert who specializes in helping business owners quickly shift their subconscious blocks to create more money and more success. Alicia has been referred to as the 'go-to hypnotherapist for entrepreneurs' and has, for over a decade, helped thousands of clients and customers break through self-imposed limitations and achieve their personal and professional goals.

Website: *www.aliciacramer.com*

BRANDY KNIGHT

THE CULT OF PLANET EARTH

Right now, people all over the planet are riddled with fear. They are sleep deprived out of this fear. They are making low-vibe choices out of this fear. They are turning on and rejecting their loved ones out of this fear. They are isolated out of this fear. They are making themselves sick out of this fear. They are losing themselves out of this fear.

This feels like a battle. A battle for our consciousness. A battle that has been going on for a very, very long time, and you are here now to help save the planet and humanity.

This fear that has attempted to take over the planet has been planted by forces that oppose the brilliance of the ultimate creative life force. These opposing forces are well versed in emotional manipulation, hypnotic brainwashing, and energetic alchemy.

Please take a long, deep breath right now before reading further. Fully inhale and fully exhale. Good job.

You are stepping into your remembering. You are stepping into your destiny. There is no more time to prolong your awakening. You signed a soul contract and chose your unique mission in this life, and we stand expanded together. We are the Light Workers.

The true alchemy of this life experience is protected by a light code. In the wrong hands, it can defiantly wreak havoc; however, only a fraction of the power will be available to anyone using these technologies with sinister intent. Often, the application of these alchemical technologies will look similar, whether they are applied by the opposing force or the creative life force. The key ingredient is the intent. The driving force and the fuel make all the difference. For example, in my practice with my clients, we often use anger release exercises like screaming and punching a pillow, working with the elements and going into a deep meditative trance. To a fly on the wall, these techniques might look identical to techniques used by opposing forces. It is the mission that is the biggest difference in the work of the Light Worker. The driving force of my work is to bring myself and others back home to self, to truth, and to love. From there, anything is possible.

Okay, so check it out: we could say that since the dawn of creation, an opposing force has been seeping its way into vulnerable young souls. It was discovered early on that fear is one of, if not the top, ways to control and brainwash living beings. Some of the ways that these sinister magicians brainwash living beings are through hypnosis, electromagnetic and acoustic wave adjustments, and emotional manipulation. If it calls to you, let yourself discover, on your own, what you need to know about the depth of the brainwashing that has occurred over time, as that is a personal journey that contributes greatly to your specific mission. Chances are this is not your first lifetime waking up to this. Keep in mind that just as a sideshow magician uses distraction tactics to perform believable illusions, the sinister opposing forces use these same methods.

I would like to go over a few key points so you have some foundational tools to feel more embodied in your mission.

Now let's go over a couple of spirituality myths that have plagued the New Age scene with a bunch of bullshit. There is quite a lot of nonsense out there about ego and neutrality. It has been widely taught that ego is something to get rid of and that neutrality means zero emotional expression. This approach has not only given the New Age and Spiritual scene a bad rap but has greatly harmed the practitioners. Ego is our friend. It is such a huge and important part of us. It's our personality and what makes us uniquely us. When we suppress what is uniquely us, we cause massive disease within our system. We want to keep the ego. So what is truly meant by eradicating ego is eradicating self-doubt and outdated belief systems. When we do this, we can truly allow a full expression of our personality to shine in an updated current time and space kinda way. How we do this can be complex. If this is new for you and/or you feel over-whelmed, please reach out to a healing arts specialist for guidance. You are not alone.

The misstep with neutrality has caused so much harm over the years. People have caused immense illness by suppressing their emotions for the sake of what they thought might achieve enlightenment. My heart hurts for these misguided beings who, knowing that there is something more to existence, ended up taking the wrong turns to get there. True neutrality is the ability to see all things from a higher perspective. We can only achieve that higher perspective if we are not tethered down by backlogged emotions. Full responsible emotional expression is a number one ingre-dient in preparing for your mission. Most of us not only have our own backlogged emotions to purge but a lineage worth of shadow to sift through and release. I strongly invite you to make responsible emotional release a top priority. Some of us need a practitioner there with us to guide us through the shadow. Others might do this on their own. Get real with yourself and ask for what you need to move this out of your system so you can achieve true neutrality. When we are free and adept with our expression, we can harness massive power and create deliberate energetic projections. The higher realms of intelligence will then be accessible to us. Releasing your emotions can be scary, especially because we have been brainwashed out of our birthright to express. It is important to under-stand that responsible emotional expression takes a daily dedicated prac-tice within a safe space. If this is new to you and/or you are feeling overwhelmed, please reach out to an emotional release specialist for guid-ance. You are not alone.

Please take another long, deep breath. Fully inhale and fully exhale. Good job.

A natural segway into accountability invites you to consider that the assholes in your life doing crazy shit are there because you invited them in. Yep! All that shit that hits the fan and you wonder why... well, you made that. In addition, you called in all the beautiful things in your life as well. Whether you remember or not, you signed a contract to be lucky enough to make your way into a human body on planet earth. That is a huge undertaking that comes with massive responsibility. All the suffering, trauma, abuse, and other shit that might suck or is beautiful is a gift you called in for yourself. The mission of a legit Light Worker requires massive energetic resources, which can only be created by waking up fully to the intricate workings of existence. Deep accountability will help get you there. We must take full accountability for everything in our life because it is a superpower. Accountability opens up massive potential within us to create and command from the highest perspectives.

For reasons, lessons, and karmic debt, known and unknown, you came here to learn and grow. A huge part of that learning process is looking into that universal mirror. By Law of Attraction, we call in all things. If you are calling in the assholes, it doesn't necessarily mean that you are an asshole to other people. Often, these complex opportunities to take full accountability show up because you are being an asshole to yourself. We were taught from a young age to treat others the way we want to be treated. What kind of backward people-pleasing bullshit is that? I mean by all means be loving and kind-hearted, but seriously, the name of the game is to treat yourself the way you want to be treated by others. That level of self-love must be the foundation of relations. The art of accountability can take a massive amount of re-framing your life story. If this is new to you and/or you feel overwhelmed, please reach out to an accountability coach for support. You are not alone.

Now, here is the big question: whose thoughts are you thinking? With the advancements of technology, hypnotic brainwashing tactics are easier than ever to penetrate your system. Our brains are like a radio ready to be tuned into a station of your choosing. The warlike tactics being used today can make it extremely challenging to even know if the station you are tuned into is even yours.

How we are focused, both consciously and subconsciously, determines what radio station we are tuned into. That station sends a thought-form to the radio. That thought-form creates an emotional experience, just like how music can create an emotional experience. The radio then broadcasts the station's transmission *vibrationally* from your system, turning the electrical wave (in the brain) into an acoustic wave (outside the brain), and there you have it! A physical manifestation created by you as a vessel of creation. Think for a moment about what your favorite and least favorite type of music is. Got it? Okay, good. Those sinister opposing forces mentioned earlier are attempting to weaken your ability to tune your radio dial yourself. One way this is happening is by literally manipulating EMF and radio waves (to name a few) with hypnosis and other fuckery. Another is by the repetition of fear consumption that seems to be broadcast all over the place. If you are focused on fear or any low-lying lack of perspective, it is like having your radio tuned into a station that plays your least favorite music over and over. This means that the physical manifestations you are creating for yourself are not gonna be that awesome. We must have command over our radio dial. As a Light Worker, this is critical.

To be sure that you are thinking thoughts you have chosen to receive, a dedicated alchemy application practice is required. You must experience what it is to tap into the highest forms of intelligence so you can get the information that is required to fulfill your life's mission. This does not mean that the shit won't hit the fan. Remember, all that shit is there for you to learn, grow and upgrade your navigation skills. To fulfill your mission, you must do your best to make sure that the shit that hits the fan will indeed serve your highest and best.

Please take a long, deep breath. Fully inhale and fully exhale. Good job.

Sometimes I think that it's beneficial to consider that no one is coming to save us. That no one is coming because they are already here. It is us, the Light Workers. It is you. You have arrived on planet earth in human form. The amount of energy and orchestration that took place to get you here is wild! Sometimes, pressure is our friend and kicks our butts into full swing.

According to Kundalini Yogic Science and Technology, the word 'God' represents the ultimate energetic force of 'Generate, Organize, Deliver or Destroy'. You are God and God is you. There is no separation between you and the ultimate creative life force. This might be a challenge to accept. That's ok. Let it be challenging. Most religions have brainwashed us into thinking that we are less than, that we are born of sin, and a bunch of other fear-based mind control bullshit, so this might take time to accept. The connection of you and God being one is something to experience. This cannot be achieved by the work of the mind alone. You must feel the creative force within and experience your power being one with the ultimate creative energy.

Just like the Law of Gravity and the Law of Attraction, there is also the Law of Polarity. On this planet, there is a natural and organic negative to the positive. That essentially means that when shit is awesome, some shit is not. What that also means is that it is a futile mission to get everyone on the planet to do the same things in the same ways and think the same thoughts and so on. There is so much to learn from each other's differences. There is so much beauty and growth to experience when we can achieve the ability to be okay with what's different, to be okay with getting out of our comfort zone, and being okay with being inaccurate sometimes. The sinister forces on this planet and their well-seasoned cult tactics might have the wool of fear pulled over your eyes. If so, you are not alone in that. This concept that everyone needs to be on the same page or else blah blah blah is simply not true. These Laws are considered as such because that they just are. It just is. Or is it?

"What comes up must come down," so the saying goes. Well, what if there was a technology that, when applied, might bypass these Laws? What if that technology has gotten into the wrong hands? What if the weapons used in the war of consciousness are not the weapons we are used to? Is that possible? If it is, that might mean we can use similar technologies to push back and rise as Light Workers. To understand how to step into our destiny and fulfill our mission. To use the driving force of love and passion to harness enough energy to potentially bend time and space as we know it. Is that possible? Well, if thoughts manifest into physical reality, I say, yes, it might be possible. Most of us require a bit of proof to truly turn a thought pattern into a belief and to create new neural pathways. That is where experiencing the subtle realms comes in. To experience yourself as God. To see God not only in you but in all. Even if those opposing forces might not have an actual soul any longer, we called them into our experience to fulfill our mission. It is the leverage we need to commit and grind. To save this planet, we humans, and potentially all existence known and unknown.

Please take a long, deep breath. Fully inhale and fully exhale. Good job.

So now that you are here and waking up to your mission, let us go over dedication and commitment. Because we live on a physical plane, you must take physical action. Having a daily practice that incorporates the development of embodied authenticity, responsible emotional release, deep accountability, genuine neutrality, and thought command is the commitment required to propel you into ascension.

The Amrit Vela translates to the *Ambrosial Period.* It is a special time, used by Yogi and alchemists, in which portals between dimensions are more available to us. The day and/or evening is fresh and new. The angels of the sun and moon to planet earth create a slipstream for us to step into our destiny. The hours between 3:00 am and 6:00 am, 4:00 am to 7:00 am, and 4:00 pm to 7 pm have been celebrated since the beginning of time as the ultimate time for connection and receptivity. I am going to share a daily recipe with you. If it feels inflow for you, I invite you to give it a shot. You will probably soon begin to know what your unique daily recipe will be and can create your own using the highest quality alchemical technologies driven by a force rooted in love.

Setting the stage for your day is a pro move. Remember that everything here is a suggestion intended to offer you an education on what can be possible. I highly advise you to be under the guidance of professional practitioners while you find your footing and beyond.

Daily rituals suggestions:

Wake up between 3:00 am and 4:00 am.
Dry-brush your body, followed by an almond oil rubdown. There are

roughly a zillion tutorials on dry-brushing swimming around the internet.

Hop in a cold shower. This can get the blood and lymph moving and grooving.

Incorporate some movement and breathwork. I highly suggest Kundalini Yoga followed by thirty-one minutes to two-and-a-half hours of mantra chanting.

Consider taking a nap to call in the lucid and prophetic dreams. Messages from the great teachers that have made their transition often come through at this time.

Wake up and fuel your system with high-quality healthy nourishment.

Carve out a safe and responsible space in the morning to get your rage and anger out.

Allow the tears to flow if needed.

End your morning practice by loving up your body and joyously expanding your chest and reaching for the sky.

Bust out some dance moves.

Let your personality shine through throughout the day.

Inspire the fuck out of others by courageously being yourself.

Take a quick nap if you need it.

Carve out time to do some sound, movement, and breathwork throughout your day.

Have fun and be bold.

End your day with a quick Yoga set and chant some mantras between 4:00 pm to 7:00 pm.

Love up your body and celebrate how fucking beautiful you are.

Hit the hay early so you can rock it out again in the morning.

These *suggested* daily rituals can be adjusted by all means. Find the alchemical technology that feels best for you, then commit to it. Every day. This is training. You must be in command of your mind. You must be in command of your body. You must be in command of the energy within and around you. You must be in command of your soul. Those that are trapped in the current cult of planet earth with the wool of fear pulled over their eyes could use our help to wake up.

You are here to wake up. You are here to step into your destiny. You are here to create a safe space for the incoming generations. You are here to help the children. You are here for Mama Earth. You are here so our souls can ascend. You are here to call in the Aquarian Age. You are here as a Light Worker. We stand expanded together, wide awake with love, integrity and passion fueling our journey.

Good job!

ABOUT THE AUTHOR

Brandy Knight, the *Esoteric Exorcist*, is an Accountability Coach, Emotional Release Specialist, Kundalini Yogic Alchemist, International Best-Selling Author, Public Speaker, CEO of Inner Caulling LLC and mother to her Light Worker baby. Her dedication to being an embodied leader, her no-bullshit approach to showing up and her crass sense of humor attracts future leaders who are ready to walk through the deep shadows, step into their destiny and have some fun doing it. The driving force fueling Brandy's work is to provide guidance to powerful people who feel lost on this planet so they can create the lasting legacy they are meant to. You can find out more about Brandy and her work at her website.

Website: *www.innercaulling.com*

1 2

CHARLI FELS

THE PATH TO NON-NEGOTIABLE LOVE

Before you read this chapter, grab some Frankincense and Spearmint Essential Oils and inhale these powerful oils. Frankincense is the Oil of Truth, revealing untrue deceptions and limitations, and also revealing to you, truth. Spearmint is the Oil of Clarity, releasing the blockages and encouraging your voice to be heard. These oils assist in accessing your inner light, speaking your truth with clarity and confidence. Take a few moments to breathe deeply, relax the body, and still the mind. Anchor your energy, connect to your soul and open your heart. As you read this chapter, allow the mind, body and soul to expand and rise.

~

T ran. I ran for my life. I was scared. A monster of a man met us in the hallway. My parents yelled, a lot. My father swinging his arms around. Did he hit my mother? I was so young, a wee little girl. Confused. Scared. This little girl with snow-white hair was such a beautiful thing. This world seemed so unpredictable, confusing, under-nourished, lonely, an isolated place for a five-year-old to experience. I was trying to make sense of my world. Subconscious reality was forming in the mind of a wee little five-year-old girl.

Is it true... that men are cruel? Men are to be feared. Men controlled women. Men overpowered women. Men are the boss. Men are superior. Men don't love from the heart. Men kept you small. Men squashed your dreams. Men un-empowered females. Men treated women as objects. Men used women to serve them. Is it true? I asked my inner child.

I heard my mother yelp of hurt. I heard loud voices. I heard silence, too. My mother would often give us non-verbal gestures, her finger to her lips … *shhh*. 'Don't make a noise. Don't upset your father. Just be quiet girls.'

I ran so fast my life depended on it. That day, there was a verbal and physical explosion. That's what it felt like for a young child. I ran behind my mother's legs; the arguing; the chaos; the screams; the voices that got louder and louder, bursting to the eardrums. I heard the stomping of heavy work boots; the air penetrated with the smell of beer and cigarettes. There was a commotion.

My father left us.

We didn't see him again for a few years.

I was attending school by then.

My mother had no money.

My mother divorced.

I lived with feeling ashamed for who I was, where I lived, how we lived.

I felt ashamed to be living in poverty. I felt ashamed that I didn't belong in a two-parent family. I felt ashamed that my parents were divorced. I felt ashamed. I never knew the emotion of shame existed until I started to explore the path of healing, as an adult. I didn't know how to feel. I didn't know how to put feelings into words. I didn't understand. *Why can't I express how I feel?*

Growing up in a home where emotions were denied and never acknowledged, it was challenging, as a little girl, to learn, understand, experience, or even manage one's own emotions. Growing up, I probably only ever knew three words on my emotional thermometer: Love. Hate. Sad.

I loved my bunny. It was a blue hand-knitted, slender body, pointy ears, two black stitched crosses for the eyes. Bunny travelled everywhere with me, slept with me, ate with me, bathed with me, rode my bike with me.

I hated people telling me what to do.

I felt sad and lonely most of the time.

I spent most of my life emotionally numbed out, decades of adulthood crippled with numbness. I didn't know how to feel. If you don't know how to feel, you don't know how to love. And when you don't know how to love, you can't possibly know how to sustain relationships, let alone the relationship with yourself.

My heart ached for love.

What is it about love? I wondered.

What does 'love' yourself really mean?

Do I need to love myself?

Who says that's what you need to do anyway, to conquer this world?

I was raised in the late 60s and 70s. The concept of love was foreign to me. It was forbidden to acknowledge that one loved thy self. Never spoken. Those who could explicitly and provocatively express self-love were seen as ego-driven, with a narcissistic attitude and disposition. It was something to feel ashamed of. As a child, I hadn't a clue that it really was quite appropriate to love yourself. Suppressing feelings was pretty normal for me.

LOST IN FEAR

Open your heart,
Let yourself in.
Let others in.
You've been a closed book for far too long.

Unravelling the layers
Where did they come from?
Childhood dreams
Childhood perceptions
Spilling into adulthood.

Living with fear,
Running with fear,
Will you stop running?
See the light.
Your heart has shrunk.
The juices squeezed out.

I'm confused.
What is love?
How do you love?
Show me love.

It's always been about love.

My Dear Heart, where are you?
My sweetheart, I've been yearning for you for so long.
Can someone help me?
I'm lost.

No, no, no.
It's like an explosion that's firing inside my head.
It's painfully full.
I can't anymore.
The mind is spinning,
Around and around,
Faster and faster,
Where's my body, where's my soul?
Stop, Stop,
Stop this, you beast.
Let me go, Ego.

I can't seem to find you
I can't see you.
I remember the beat,
The sweetness of your beat,

The tenderness of your rhythm.

Despair and distortion.
My eyes are scanning the room.
I've lost you.
Who has taken you?
No, not you again!
Go to sleep, ego-mind.
I want to feel the beat,
The beat of me.

I miss you,
I want connection,
I need my soul.
My heart.

THE MERRY-GO-ROUND

The first toy I ever bought my daughter was a 'Jack in the Box'. Wind up the music, a crescendo and pop! Out jumps Jack. Sorry, Jack, I'm pushing you back down into your little box and slamming the lid down. Let me try that again. I enjoyed slamming that lid and keeping him quiet. I will control, I will decide when I will let you emerge again. So often throughout my life, I have been shut down, the lid slammed down just to keep me quiet, unseen, unheard. The thoughts, triggers and behaviours of others determining my destiny. Ouch!

Are you waiting passively, hiding quietly down in the box until someone opens your lid?

Is someone controlling your life strings?

I'd like to ask you: what are you waiting for?

Waiting for the world to explode?
Waiting for the pandemic to go away?
Waiting to get thin?
Waiting to be fit and active?

Waiting for your hair to grow wild?
Waiting for your partner to come home and start living?
Waiting for your dog to approach you and lick you with love?

I look at my phone; I wait with anticipation to hear it ding.
I'm waiting; I'm on the edge of my chair,
Waiting to see who contacts me,
Who reaches out to me,
Who acknowledges my existence,
Who tells me I'm doing amazingly!

I'm waiting to be recognised.
I'm waiting to be validated.
I'm waiting for someone to tell me I'm doing a good job.
I'm waiting for someone to say yes.
I'm waiting for my bank account to grow.
I'm waiting.

Why am I waiting?

I sit still,
I ponder.
What am I doing?
I could do a million things
I should do a million things
But
I don't
I just sit and wait.

THE WAITING GAME

Who's playing the waiting game with me?
What's it teaching you?
The mind dances,

Dances with the ego.

The waiting game manifests.
I wait.
I'm still, I listen, I hear the birds chirp,
The humming of human activity.
I feel the air.
Stop the mind chatter.
Focus on the heart.
It feels so tight, like the perfect formation of a rosebud.
The petals strangling each other, so tightly.
I can't breathe.

The days continue.
I wait some more.
The outer petals start to fray around the edges,
They wiggle and squirm.
This tight suffocation of this heart commences to open.
My heart opens.
A slow release.
A release of joy.
A smile.
The body softens.

I listen,
To my heart.
You are significant, my darling.
Believe in YOU
You don't need to wait anymore.
You've got this.
You
It's all about you.
You are SIGNIFICANT.
Time to unleash.
Time to be unapologetic.

Listen and the divine will guide you.
Notice what you're listening to.
Be still, listen, and you shall see the greatest LOVE.

I have always been active in carving my own path. But what is it about this particular moment in time? Why am I hesitating? Fear lingers. Day after day, the self-doubt manifests. I fear judgement, shame, imposter syndrome, unworthiness, unprotected, resentful, disconnected, inadequate, hopelessness.

It's the spiral of the ego-mind that keeps you small, that restricts you.

Seriously, my darling, are you happy being small? You're shivering, meek and weak.

FOLLOW YOUR PATH

Step up and take control of your life. See your vision, feel your vision.

You have the power.

You can stir the most amazing emotions to tingle your body and soul.

Energise your soul.
Smile.
You are amazing!
God has given you a gift.
See it, my love.
Embrace the love for you.
Accept yourself.
Smile at this gift.
You are one in a million.

You are special.
Recognise this, my darling.
The path your life takes starts with you.
Take that step of loving you. Follow that path. It's long but follow the path.

Look straight ahead, not sideways.

Breathe deeply and still the mind. Sit still, my love and feel.
Your journey has been going on for so long.
Battled from side to side, tossed around and around,
Sounds of judgement, hatred, anger, confusion, chaos, guilt, shame, the victim.

Lost in translation, the ego grabbed your thoughts,
Twisted and turned you about.
Chaos, heartache, suffering.
She survives and so do you.

Follow the path, little girl. It will take you home.

It's time to shed the tears.
It's time to follow the heart.
It's time to follow the divine path.
What is it saying to you?
Are you listening hard enough?
What is it telling you?
Look out for breadcrumbs; they are the signs to lead you through your journey into the Golden Age.

Just follow it and great riches will follow you.
It's time to come home, little one.
No longer will you be lost.
The true you will be revealed, don't fight it. We see you, my darling.

TRIUMPH

It's YOU who leads into the Golden Age. The non-negotiable truth of self-love. This non-negotiable soulful act is the key to pathing your way into the future. This, my dearest, is your triumph. Your opening of the blossom, casting aside the unworthiness, shame and doubt. Walk the delight

117

of love, of life, to find the ultimate you. Nothing is impossible. Love leads. Love leads through the heart, not the mind. There will not be one unopened petal that holds fear.

You must surrender. Surrender the ego-mind, surrender the control over your mind, body and soul.

This, my dearest, brings access to the spiritual power of divine fulfilment. Trust that your love is magnificent, significant and just right. It is the work of your love and soul.

Open the heart and surrender into the Golden Age. Surrender your heart and soul to your God and give forth total trust. Be comfortable with the unknown, celebrate with the soul of the unknown path. Your source will reveal exactly what is needed to move forward.

Let the heavens open and pour the gift of love into your body and soul.

Love. Surrender. Trust. My gorgeous one.

ABOUT THE AUTHOR

Charli Fels is an International Best-Selling Author; the Creator of Strutology, and the CEO and founder of OSTRICH180 Publishing a hybrid publishing house flipping traditional publishing on its head, designing author success through strategic brand building and positioning as expert authority. OSTRICH180 Publishing specialises in non-fiction, soul-stirring poetry and multi-author books for innovative and creative entrepreneurs.

As a world-leading Identity Designer, the Art of Feminine Presence Coach, Scientific Hand Analyst, and Early Childhood Educator, Charli applies a holistic approach to personal branding through studying the Brand's State of Being. This is the mind, body and soul of the brand. She is known for her innovative mindset, practices and approach to life and business. Working with the most exciting Leaders and Entrepreneurs, she empowers the strut to evolve, embodying the inner icon, aligning the true genius and stepping into the audacious power; for designing your success is designing your very own Strutosphere.

As a mother of two daughters, one with a disability; decades working with students and clients, Charli has witnessed the growth and power when one surrenders and releases past limiting beliefs and stories, trusts the source and one's internal connection. Through Charli's own inner wrestles and healing, she audaciously gives permission for soul expression and stands for the unleashing of voices.

Website: *www.ostrich180.com*
Email: *info@ostrich180.com*

13

GEORGINA EL MORSHDY

HOW YOUR MESSAGE CAN HEAL YOURSELF AND THE WORLD

Why do you believe you're here—
at *this* time, in *these* times, and *for* these times?

I f you're impact-driven, you likely have a mission to spark change in the world. If so, your message is key because it conveys the possibility you hold for the people you best serve.

But how do we discover our soul's message?

I've found that the answer lies at the intersection of who you are, what life has taught you, and what you're naturally gifted at. What I call the journey to find your YOU.

Here's why...

When you know your true self, you can show your whole self. When you understand what life has taught you, you can see how you're uniquely positioned to impact. When you leverage your soul's gifts, you do your best work effortlessly.

It's why the self-discovery journey to your message unlocks more than marketing words alone. It sparks the courage to know you matter, the strength to own your uniqueness, and the self-love to be fearlessly visible with your brilliance.

No wonder the path to YOU is confronting and uncomfortable, but as Marianne Williamson said, *"Our deepest fear is not that we are inadequate. Our deepest fear is that we are powerful beyond measure."*

The truth is, most of us weren't raised on a diet of self-love. Instead, society conditioned us to look outside for validation and acceptance. It's why many people feel conflicted to own their gifts or be seen in their power. We weren't raised on introspective or reflection either, which means we can struggle to trust our intuition, inner guidance, and individual wisdom.

As a result, we become disconnected from our inner knowing, stray from our soul's path, and find it a challenge to know how we can make a difference in the world.

But what if your life's calling is to work your way back to YOU?

I've always known I was here to do something meaningful. I imagine you feel the same way.

As a child, I was an ambitious big thinker with wild dreams. I remember being outspoken and extroverted. Bold with my ideas, and confident in my abilities, I had an essence that was hard to ignore!

It was clear I had potential, but there was also a lot to learn. I needed to balance my bulldozing desire to lead with listening, tolerance, and collaboration. Maybe this was why the bullies showed up?

My teenage years eroded that confident child. I was picked on for being bossy and big-headed. I was ridiculed for my acne, large forehead, and glasses. The bullying got so bad I was forced to move schools.

The experience changed me. My self-worth plummeted and that fiery, fierce child became a shadow of her former self. I loathed the way I looked and hated myself for it. Fuelled by the expectation that people wouldn't like me, I became socially awkward and insular. I silenced my voice, kept my ideas to myself, and started pouring my heart into journals.

In the process, I lost my ability to express my true self, and it took two awakenings to bring it back.

The first time, I was twenty-five. It was 2001—the dawn of a new millennium—and I was busy trying to make my mark on the world.

I'd achieved my childhood dream of being one of the first in my family to graduate. I'd achieved a brilliant job with great career prospects and a generous pension. I was climbing the corporate ladder successfully, but inside, I was crumbling with self-inflicted pressure.

At work, the praise rolled in. I'd been headhunted and promoted, but I couldn't see the brilliance others valued. I couldn't own my strengths either. Unknowingly, I'd programmed myself to expect a re-run of my childhood experiences and believed rejection or criticism was lurking around every corner.

To push off this inevitable moment of rejection, I created a world where I wasn't allowed to get anything wrong. As a result, I lived in fear of making a mistake and would constantly imagine worst-case scenarios where my actions led to a major disaster! The stress was overwhelming. Frequent panic attacks caused chest pains and difficulties breathing. There were plenty of days I didn't want to wake up and many more when I longed to hide in bed.

I hid my challenges well. On the surface, I looked like any other successful, twenty-something, but eventually, the anxiety broke me. I was diagnosed with depression, prescribed antidepressants, and referred for counselling.

Back then, mental health issues were a stigma. A part of me was ashamed that I'd fallen apart, but the wiser me knew this breakdown was *exactly* what I needed.

Rumi said, *"the wound is the place where the light gets in."*

My counsellor helped me see that *I'd* created the scenarios that drove me to my knees. It was a relief to know the fear was self-made and the brutal voice wasn't my truth. Instead, it was a reaction to the bullying, self-loathing, and visibility wounding I'd carried for so long.

In other words, life could be different.

This revelation caused something unfamiliar to move inside me. I desired more from life and became inquisitive about who I really was. The realms of spirituality and personal growth offered the answers I craved so I jumped in.

I became a seeker, attending all the workshops, courses, and events I could get my hands on. I wanted to understand life more deeply. I longed to know why my heart felt so closed. I was curious to explore why I felt so damaged and why I was so fearful of myself.

I had a big breakthrough while jumping among the buzzing crowd of 8,000 people at London's Excel Centre. I was at the Tony Robbins Unleash The Power Within seminar.

The voice inside said, *"You're here to help people... and one day, you'll be on a platform inspiring others to find themselves - so they too can make a difference in this world."*

It all felt ridiculous! The vision was so far removed from my current reality! At the time, I had zero helping skills, minimal self-confidence, and I was healing depression.

But a channel had cracked open, and life would never be the same again.

My family thought I was crazy to quit my corporate career and leave the conventional path. On the surface, it looked as though I'd thrown away everything I'd worked so hard to achieve. But the deeper voice reassured me that complementary therapies would take me closer to my true path.

And they did...

I spent most of 2004 acquiring helping skills thanks to my complementary therapy training. I was buzzing with the vibe of newness and took the opportunity to study NLP, life coaching, and energy healing too. I also explored tarot and astrology and ran a monthly circle for a group of friends where we shared insights, ideas, and conversations. This year was transformative on a physical, emotional, and spiritual level. My inner voice grew more loving, my spiritual connection deepened, and my self-awareness heightened.

I reclaimed lost parts of myself and new doors opened. I was invited to teach by the college that taught me—so I did. During the summer break of

2005, I felt a strong pull to travel to Dahab in Egypt to invest in some introspective writing time. Instead, I met my husband! We got married in 2006, had our first daughter, and moved back to my hometown of Plymouth, UK, where I continued developing my teaching career.

Through this work, I built my confidence and got clearer on my passions and skills. I was finding deeper answers, doing purposeful work, and feeling better in my skin. I was also trusting my intuition more so when the voice demanded more time freedom after my second daughter was born in 2010, I listened.

During my maternity leave, I trained to be a freelance copywriter and transitioned out of teaching. It felt incredible to monetise my life-long passion for writing. As a professional writer, I felt a sense of completeness and fulfilment that I'd not had before.

I felt confident this *was* the work I was born to do. Finally, I could stop the incessant searching and focus fully on being a parent and building my business. I cleared out my spiritual books, quit reading cards, forgot my crystals, and declared to the universe that I was done seeking.

The channel closed and the deeper voice inside fell silent.

Copywriting was a perfect career for me. The work was purposeful and I thrived on the creativity it inspired. Thanks to the clients I attracted, I got to share potent messages and promote products I loved and used myself.

I joined up more personal dots too. I saw how years of social awkwardness had cultivated an invaluable gift. I had an instinctive knack for asking questions that cracked clients open. Combined with the soul-deep listening I'd mastered as a way to avoid talking about me, clients could access inspired ideas and insights about themselves and their message. This work was exhilarating! It felt amazing to be leading trans-formative conversations that elevated my clients and their work in the world.

As feedback for this gift rolled in, I felt my soul work stretch beyond copywriting. It was no longer enough for me to write words alone. I wanted to activate voices and help leaders craft messages and visions for building a new paradigm.

But what surprised me most was that one of the voices I desired to amplify was mine. This was the beginning of my second awakening—the deep knowing that I had something important to say too.

A light had switched on and the channel had reopened. I could see how my unique pattern of life experiences had led *directly* to this expanded realm of work, visibility, and impact.

It all made sense. The desire for leadership and the big impact I had as a child. The introspection and journaling I'd learned as a bullied teenager. The empathy, listening, and healing I'd practiced as a complementary therapist. The visibility and teaching skills I'd mastered as a teacher. The power to use words to inspire action as a copywriter.

I'd also walked the path that helped me to understand what it takes to be visible with who you are and what you know. I'd been the person who overlooked, undermined, and denied my brilliance—because I was afraid of being seen by people who might judge or hurt me.

I knew the pain of staying silent and the sheer pleasure of being seen and heard for who you really are. I'd walked the path from visibility to invisibility and back again. I'd learned how to crack myself open to access individual wisdom and get clarity on my life's purpose. I'd walked the path of transforming my self-worth so I could feel confident making a stand for what I believe.

Thanks to my unique mix of experiences and skills, wrapped up in my personality, it was clear I was born for visibility and message-making work.

I launched Find Your YOU in 2016 and used this platform to spread the word that who you are is just as important as what you know. In the age of information abundance, knowledge is no longer scarce—it's at our fingertips. In turn, people aren't looking for answers alone. They're choosing WHO they want to learn from.

I also used this platform as a space to share myself and my message more visibly.

This decision helped me heal my visibility wounds further. It's one thing to stand up and share knowledge as a teacher. You have a curriculum and textbooks to 'hide' behind. It's one thing to share someone else's message that you believe in—because they are the face that gets seen, not yours! It's another thing entirely to remove your social mask and declare, *"this is who I am."*

I still remember the fear I felt when I began sharing my stories and individual wisdom. I felt so exposed and vulnerable. My heart raced and my palms sweated. I felt nauseous and overwhelmed by the discomfort that filled my body. I'd go to hit publish, only to stop myself over and over. When I finally had the courage to put the piece live, I'd have to leave my office because I couldn't hold the energy!

But step-by-step, I encouraged myself to honour my gifts, and as my confidence grew, I got bolder with my message and visibility.

In April 2020, I launched the Writing Your Best Self podcast for Best-Self Co. We publish weekly tips and interviews about finding yourself through journaling and deep-dive conversations.

In October 2021, I completed a year of consecutive Facebook lives, which fulfilled my intention of sharing my individual wisdom with my voice, not just written content.

I started running online programmes [leveraging my teaching experience] and providing one-to-one consulting to help visionaries find their soul message and awaken the potent messenger within. I also created a series of inner journey tools to help people use introspection and journaling for personal growth and inspired content ideas.

Today, Find Your YOU has evolved into a brand that empowers impact-driven entrepreneurs and visionary leaders to explore their inner world and find their authentic message—so they can be fearlessly visible with the work they came here to do.

I love how my work draws upon all the skills, experiences, and knowledge I've collected over the years. Everything from journaling, to teaching, writing, and creating spaces for transformation is all woven into my unique blend of impact. It's divine perfection! If you join up the dots of your life, you discover you have everything you need to do your very best work.

And while I've come this far, I'm not yet done—because finding YOU and sharing that message is the work of your lifetime.

When you know that your message is your greatest personal growth catalyst and your unique gift to the world, there are always more layers to peel away!

It's a growth catalyst because your message pulls you into the vortex of your fullest expression. It inspires you to overcome your visibility wounds, trust yourself deeply, and create the space to be an embodiment of what you teach.

And your message is your unique gift to the world because what you've figured out about life is someone else's shortcut. It's someone else's inspiration. Someone else's activation. Your successes show others what's possible, and your failures serve as a reminder that you can rise out of the darkness stronger, smarter, and more evolved than ever.

In short, who you are and what you do creates an embodied blueprint for navigating the microcosm of the universe that you've figured out.

It's why your message holds the potential to heal yourself and change the world.

~

As we head into 2022 and beyond, a desire to find your message couldn't be more divinely timed.

I believe humanity is headed towards a crossroads. Our options could range between extinction of our species or evolution of our collective consciousness. This sounds dramatic, but sometimes we need extreme external pressures to call out the best in us.

There's a growing urge to replace outdated structures and systems with a society that works for more people and the planet. Thankfully, people are rising up with new visions and possibilities. We're challenging each other and ourselves. We're asking new questions and sparking different conversations.

Life *knows* we're at a tipping point.

It also knows that each of us can play a part in determining what happens next—because we all have a soul-inspired message to embody and share.

You can make a difference by understanding what life has taught you about life - and then sharing that. You can elevate the collective vibe by investing in your own inner work to heal, evolve, and elevate yourself.

It's as Meister Eckhart, the 14th-century Christian mystic, said:

"The outer work can never be small if the inner work is great. And the outer work can never be great if the inner world is small."

Right now, there are people waiting to hear what you have to say, simply because of who you are. You hold a missing piece of their life's jigsaw, and they're waiting for your lighthouse to switch on so they can find it.

So don't hold back - even if you see others speaking on similar topics.

If the message hasn't been spoken by you, there's still more to say.

No one can share through the same lens as you. No one else on this planet has the same unique tapestry of stories, philosophies, life lessons, values, or beliefs as you—because they are not you.

This is the Age of the Individual Messenger, a time for sparking impact through your voice, visibility, and vibe. Through your individuality, you can attract an aligned audience, create products and services you love, and express your message in the way only you can, whether that's through writing, speaking, poetry, dance, art, or music etc.

So let your message-making empower you to grow as a human, evolve as a soul, and leave your greatest legacy as a result.

Make this season of life one where you lean deeper into YOU.

Trust in the unique pattern of experiences that life puts on your path.

Look for the external signs and listen to the messages from within.

Choose to be uncensored, untamed, and unleashed with your true essence.

In turn, you'll experience your potential, leave a legacy that lasts, and step fully into the person you came here to be.

With love,
Georgina

ABOUT THE AUTHOR

Georgina El Morshdy is the founder of *Find Your YOU*. She's also a messaging mentor, intuitive writer, a creative muse, and host of the *Writing Your Best Self* podcast.

Georgina is passionate about using message-making as a catalyst for personal growth and a tool for sparking impact. She believes that in this Age of the Individual Messenger, our individuality is one of the most potent tools we have for living an aligned, purposeful life and making a difference in the world.

Through her programmes, private coaching, and journaling tools, Georgina empowers impact-driven entrepreneurs, creatives, and vision-aries to amplify their unique voice, vision, and vibe, so they can share their soul's message with fearless visibility.

Georgina lives in Plymouth, UK, with her three children and husband. When she's not message-making, she loves journaling, creating with her singing bowls, long walks by the ocean, and deep conversations that touch your soul.

Website: www.findyouryou.co.uk
Facebook: www.facebook.com/georgina.morshdy
Podcast: www.writingyour.bestself.co

14

JOANNE MARTIN

EMPOWERING LEADERS WHO ARE POSITIVELY CHANGING THE FACE OF HUMANITY

"Whether you think you can or think you can't you're right"
- Henry Ford

I t's with this famous quote that I'd like to start you on a journey of discovery to remember who you truly are and what you're here to achieve.

You are here as a leader for humanity and have a pivotal role to play in the transformation from the existing paradigm to the Golden Age.

As timelines shift and the veil between realities thins, it is up to us to lead the way for the human collective and the generations to come. We are all incarnated on the earth at this time for a purpose, our soul purpose and it's time to step up, to rise and to be the solid foundation for all those who are navigating the world at this momentous time in history.

We are at the frontier of history, we are here to make a difference and we are here to lead others through this heavy energy and into the light.

This is why Henry Ford's quote is so pertinent right now. We are creating and manifesting our thoughts and reality at great speed. It's a case of, if you think it, you can create it. Remember that. Each thought you have creates energy and initiates the universal Law of Attraction. It's important as leaders right now to focus on love, trust and hope, to help humanity see a brighter future and proactively work towards it.

A consciousness shift for humanity has been ushered in. How we navigate this shift in the collective consciousness is directly impacted by our own level of awareness, mindset and souls journey. This period calls on us to release judgement, anger, hatred and limiting beliefs that are holding us back from achieving inner peace and true happiness. It's also about stepping into our roles as leaders, wayshowers and guides for all human beings on the planet right now.

The three greatest gifts we have right now that can help us lead into the Golden Age are our mindset, leadership capability and dream building skills. By developing and harnessing our abilities in these areas we can help lead the way towards the Great Awakening and in turn, create a brighter future for humanity.

MINDSET FOR TRANSFORMATIONAL SUCCESS

As we consider the massive shift in consciousness playing out around the globe right now, let us ponder what's important for each of us individually at this moment in time. We are exactly where we are meant to be in every moment. Each thought, decision and action we've taken has led us to exactly where we are in this now moment. Whether these things have been conscious, intentional or guided by others, each of us is still exactly where we need to be in this moment in history.

Mindset is a set of beliefs, self-perceptions and thoughts that we hold about ourselves. These elements determine our outlook on life, behaviour, attitude and the actions we take when navigating life. Proactively working on our mindset, clearing limiting beliefs, stepping outside the current paradigm and taking the path less travelled are major contributors to success and happiness.

Personally, I've always walked to the beat of my own drum, taken the path less travelled and followed my intuition to create a life I love. Whilst highly educated, with a Masters in Adult Education and multiple university qualifications, I've always taken things I've learned and incorporated my own thinking into them. It's this creativity of thought, the ability to harness innovation and create new ways of doing things that has created my biggest wins and successes to date. Importantly, it's also the drive to 'be the best I can be' that has helped me the most in navigating my life's journey. In business, I'm constantly evolving and working on my mindset whilst developing my own unique approach to business. It's this ability to step back from the busyness of life and really focus on self-development that has helped me create happiness and recognise my true life's purpose.

As you prepare to step into your role as a leader for humanity, tune into what are you experiencing, being, seeing and feeling right now. Ask yourself these questions:

- What no longer serves me?
- What beliefs, assumptions and programs can I leave behind right now?
- Intuitively, what is the best way forward?
- How can I create my own success?
- How will my success as a leader shape the future of humanity?

Reflect on your answers to these questions and take positive action to clear limiting elements that are holding you back from stepping into your role as a leader for humanity. Focus your positive intention on bringing your dreams, goals and intuitive guidance to life.

FOCUS ON YOUR MINDSET

Use this quick and effective clearing technique to help you create a greater chance of success. Practice this daily and you will notice a shift in your mindset, focus and happiness levels.

Step 1
Take a deep breath in and out, ensuring you consciously release all the negative energy, feelings and emotions swirling through every cell of your body right now.
Repeat this three times to centre your energy and ground yourself in this moment.

Step 2

Now focus on one negative emotion, feeling or belief that has been in your conscious mind today.

Take a deep breath in and repeat in your mind:

I release all positive and negative emotions with _ (negative emotion/feeling/belief) _ through all space and time.

Release your breath. Take a deep breath in and out. Repeat this process three times for each negative emotion, feeling or belief.

Step 3

If any specific negative feelings or emotions come up for you, then you can also release those subconscious beliefs by saying:

I release all _ (negative feeling or emotion) with _ (situation, relationship, context) _ through all space and time.

Here's an example to help you:

I release all fear with following my dreams through all space and time.

Remember it's important to repeat the process three times for each individual emotion, feeling or belief that you're clearing from your subconscious mind.

Step 4

It's super important to always finish this process with a touch of gratitude.

I'm so happy and grateful for all the __ (insert positive context) __ in my life.

I'm so happy and grateful for _____.

Here's an example to help get you started:

I'm so happy and grateful for everything that has worked out perfectly in my life.

The key to success with everything is to be consistent and do this daily. You'll soon notice small positive changes in your life.

LEADING INTO THE GOLDEN AGE

I've been contemplating leadership, what it means at this point in history and how leaders navigate this as humanity collectively moves forward into a new era. We're in a period of exponential growth, a releasing of the old ways of being, living and making money. As we embrace the new, how do we lead through this transformative period?

We are all here for a purpose. We're here to lead through this change as an activated way-shower, to inspire the next generation and show them the way forward. Each of you reading this book are on the planet to make the world a better place.

How are you going to lead the way for humanity?

Here are some questions to contemplate as you lead into the new age:

- How does releasing the old ways of being, impact the new ways of living?
- What does making money look like over the next twelve months, three years, seven years?
- What is the real reason I'm here at this moment in time?
- How can I lead effectively as I embrace new ways of being?
- What does saying 'yes' mean as our world transforms?

The time is now. There is no time to plan for perfection, there is no time to waste. Humanity needs you to step up now. Pure love-filled, intuitive leadership is the greatest gift we can give to the next generation. It's time to take your seat at the table. You were born for this time, to light the way for all those that follow.

TRUSTING YOURSELF AND HARNESSING YOUR LEADERSHIP SKILLS

We are at a turning point in history, that pivotal point in time where you make a conscious decision about what side of history you want to be on. Leadership is not just for politicians, CEOs and entrepreneurs. It's also the domain of a new breed of leaders, the ones creating a more sustainable, equitable and humanitarian future for the entire planet.

Leadership is a valuable, innate skill that everyone from any vocation or background has the potential to harness and use to make the world a better place. Whilst effective leadership may not come naturally for most of us, there are several methods that you can use to build and refine your leadership capability.

It's time to discover the leader within you! To share your skills, knowledge and inner knowing with the world and support the human collective through these transformational times. Here are some techniques you can use to boost your leadership skills and create a positive impact on the world:

a. Follow your intuition. Many of the great leaders who positively change history have a strong inner knowing, that gut feeling they just can't shake, that serves them well and guides their life's journey. It's time now for you to trust your inner guidance and light the way for others.

b. Harness innovation. There is always a better way to do things, an evolution of being and a way to shape a positive future for humanity. Be brave, share your wisdom, seek truth and discover new ways of doing, being, living.

c. Be present. Start each day with a short meditation, where you tune into your inner knowing and angelic guidance. Throughout the day, make time to be in touch with your senses, breathe deeply, stand on the grass and connect to the universal grounding energy.

d. Be passionate and maintain a positive attitude. Most people take cues from others in social and business situations. You can teach others to have a positive attitude and be passionate in their efforts by role modelling this behaviour yourself.
- You can energise an entire team or group by maintaining an upbeat attitude and always striving to excel. This will help ensure the collective group accomplishes more, is more motivated and demonstrates greater passion in achieving objectives.
- Effective leaders also harness more traditional leadership techniques. This provides them with a competitive advantage, allows them to connect with people at all levels and ensures they successfully enable transforma-

tional change at an organisational, community and social level. Key areas of expertise you should develop include:

I. Strive for excellence. Successful leadership is based on your ability to set the bar for yourself and others. Love, integrity, and transparency help you be a good role model for others. Seek out ways to improve yourself, expand your skills, develop new competencies and aspire to excellence.

II. Focus on your vision and set goals. Consider what you want to accomplish in different areas of your life. Set goals that will help you to achieve your vision and inspire others to do the same. Celebrate success:
- Set goals to measure your performance and progress. Encourage others to do the same and celebrate the success of all those around you.
- Create goals that can be broken down into smaller milestone goals. This will allow you to measure progress, celebrate successes and maintain motivation.

III. Identify available resources. When setting goals, always work with the resources you currently have, rather than developing plans based on resources and circumstances that you wish you had. Being realistic will keep you on track, taking positive action and achieving success. Remember goals are fluid, so it's important to refine your dreams and goals to ensure you achieve your objectives.

IV. Develop your people skills. Great leaders are known for their ability to inspire others to take positive action and work towards a common goal. To inspire others to work with you, focus on developing your people skills, intuition and emotional intelligence.
- *Learn how to listen.* Doing so helps to establish a connection, allows you to tune into your intuition, build trust and establish strong relationships with people, meaning others are more likely to follow your lead and help you.
- *Help others to be their best.* Part of being a good leader is motivating others towards positive change. A good leader doesn't take all the recog-

nition; instead, they acknowledge the contribution of their team and allow them to receive acknowledgment for a job well done.

- *Seek input from others.* When setting goals and making plans to reach your objectives, empower others to be part of the decision-making process. This ensures everyone has skin in the game and will be more motivated to help you achieve the objective.

V. Be passionate and maintain a positive attitude. Most of us take cues from others in social situations, so you can teach others to have a positive attitude and to be passionate in their efforts by doing so yourself.

- Don't underestimate the power of a positive mindset. Maintaining an upbeat attitude and striving to excel will help energise the entire team. Ensuring everyone accomplishes more and feels connected to the outcome.

Taking the time to develop your leadership skills can radically increase the amount of positive transformational change you can initiate across the planet. It will also help drive the success you experience in all areas of your personal and professional life. These tips will help you hone your leadership capability so that you can achieve your goals and help lead humanity to a brighter, more peaceful and connected future.

THE TIME TO FOLLOW YOUR DREAMS AND LEAD HUMANITY TO A BETTER FUTURE IS NOW

Dreams are the essence of life. They are at the core of your being. If you're reading this, your dreams are bigger than you. You are here to make a difference and have been provided with the talents and wisdom to achieve those dreams.

You hold the power to create a better future for humanity. Your dreams hold the keys to the future. Focus on the intuitive messages, angelic guidance and universal flow to hold your vision for a better, more peaceful, more love-filled future.

Take note of your intention. Where your intention flows, energy grows and great outcomes can be achieved. Each day, consider your dreams. What can you do today to work towards achieving the outcome you were born to deliver? Feel into your true purpose and visualise your dreams in action and as the reality you are helping to create.

Every thought and every action is shaping our future in this now moment. Remember the gift of magic, love and magic of the heart. Harness the power of thought and use it strategically to help make the world a better place. We all have the power to create the life we choose for ourselves. However, as leaders at this pivotal point in history, we have a greater responsibility to the human collective. Our role is to be the wayshowers, lightworkers and guides to create a better future for humanity.

ABOUT THE AUTHOR

Joanne Martin is an International Best-Selling Author and Book Writing Coach. She's the CEO and Founder of Golden Earth Publishing, a bespoke publishing house specialising in children's books, solo author books and manuscript development for innovative and creative entrepreneurs.

As a mother to two energetic and intuitive souls, Joanne loves children and is passionate about leaving a legacy for future generations through published literary works. She believes we have a unique opportunity to see our work in action as we create a better world for future generations.

Joanne works globally with authors to share their stories with the world, up-level their businesses, increase revenue opportunities and magnify their marketing impact through bestselling books.

Website: *www.jomartin.com*
Facebook: *www.linkedin.com/in/joannemartin33*

JOCELYN CHONG

You are the sum of your experiences. And all of them, from your first memory to your forays in industry, have been essential to your growth. They've shaped your values and beliefs, made you into the person you are. And just as importantly, *they define your uniqueness as an entrepreneur.*

I remember watching my grandparents working at their shop in Malaysia—unloading canned goods when they arrived from overseas; the way they took inventory, negotiated, ran transactions, counted coins. It was my first glimpse into entrepreneurship, and it stuck with me.

As did visits to the lolly store. My grandfather would give me a ten-cent coin every day and walk me there. I'd buy two sweets, and while I didn't know it then, I was learning the value of money.

Think back. Do you have similar memories?

It goes without saying, your experiences guide your decisions today. For better or worse. Savvy entrepreneurs will use them to their advantage, building companies based on who they are and what life has taught them.

However, the most attuned business owners take it a step further, diving deep into their beliefs and psyche to free themselves from what holds them back. *From there, unlimited abundance is yours to command.*

Choosing to be a soulful entrepreneur means levelling up. It's time to decide what you really want, and allow yourself to reach your highest potential.

When you do, working hard is less of a burden and more of a joy. In fact, you'll do twice as much with your time and have so much more fun. All it takes is boldly designing a business model that suits who you are and the lifestyle you aspire to have.

Of course, that's easier said than done. What usually happens is you pigeonhole yourself into what you're familiar with rather than what gives you *purpose*. I know because it was very much the same for me.

At seventeen, I moved from Malaysia to Australia on my own. Bringing my grandparents' work ethic with me, I applied myself to studying accounting and finance, while trying to adjust to this foreign land and a language I wasn't too great with.

For the first time, I not only had to make good grades but also look after myself. Yet, the drive never left me. I was determined to learn, explore, and excel. And so, what could've been a difficult time became a period of significant, life-changing growth instead.

After graduating, my career took off. Working as an auditor with Ernst & Young exposed me to giants like BHP, Visy Industries and ABB Grain. A few years later, I entered the world of retail banking with Westpac.

In my first two years there, I was promoted quickly. From managing more and more people to handling larger and larger amounts of money, I was constantly given greater responsibility. Soon enough, it led me into the role of Financial Planner.

However, while I was thriving professionally, my personal life was crumbling. My fiancé broke our engagement three months after proposing. No explanation, nothing.

As you can imagine, it was heartbreaking. And humbling. It took years to fully heal. Swallowing a bitter pill, processing it and allowing it to move through all facets of your being (mind, body and soul) takes time.

Especially when you don't deal with it head-on.

See, in the beginning, I put on a brave face. Rather than viewing this as an opportunity to re-evaluate my life, I poured my energy into my work. I focused on making multiple six figures and landing a promotion into the investment role I wanted. All the while actively ignoring my wound.

Until that is, I couldn't. And the pain burst through every barrier I had put up.

Still, I do believe I needed to go through all this to learn and ultimately help others in similar situations. I realised unattended wounds don't heal. The pain finds its way to bleed out and infect the other pockets of your life. "Compartmentalising," in other words, doesn't work.

The only thing that does is addressing the hurt head-on. If it's buried deep beneath layers and masks, you need to peel those back. And when you do and the pain is too strong to cope with on your own, you need to ask for help.

Just as you must in every area of your life. To be strong is not to stand alone but to accept support and direction when required. We need to co-create with the universe. And to do that, we need guides.

How many times have you heard that?

How many times have you actually taken this advice?

It took me a long time to follow my heart. For me, that led to coaching.

The idea had been building for a while. I just hadn't leaped before because my corporate life was safe, comfortable. It took my world crashing down around me before I could make a switch to let my true talents guide my way forward.

While I had always been good at my job, where I truly excelled was leading teams, helping clients grow their business or set up their practices.

There was an energy emanating between myself and those I worked with that left everyone, at the end of a session, filled with the sparkle of joy and hope. I could see it in their facial expressions, and I felt it in their collective spirits.

I chose to be a business and life coach instead because, after all that time, I understood what gave me the truest sense of fulfilment.

Of course, I needed to go through all my experiences to get to where I am now. They added to the value I can offer today. Without them, I would not have the tools that help clients quantum leap to make impactful changes and build lifestyles they are unequivocally passionate about.

The Value of Your Experience Is Immeasurable,
Provided You Use It to Your Advantage

All this goes to show how instrumental your experiences are. If that is, you harness them to their fullest potential.

How do you do that?

Use your experiences to reveal and understand your natural expertise. It's not always what you're paid to do in a job, but what comes to you intuitively—your superpowers. The things you do so readily that they never feel like a chore or burden.

Rather than relying solely on prescribed, standard business models, elevate them based on the unique value you bring. Re-envision your customer avatar and test drive your offers again and again. Patience is required to refine the research process. But it is essential to understand the problems they face, in depth.

Be warned, you will encounter challenges and days when you feel like avoiding this cycle of research and refinement. You're human. Be sure to acknowledge that while resisting the trap of thinking, "I know enough, why bother?"

You've got to be strong and train your mind to think empowering thoughts.

Download all your limiting beliefs onto paper. Ask yourself, "What's holding me back from doing the work? What am I avoiding even though I know it will get results?" Write it all down.

Now consider this: are any of these reasons supporting your values, vision and goals for your business?

Get into the habit of re-training these reasons into positive thoughts. Start by rejecting statements such as, "I don't know", "I can't", "I'm confused", "It's too hard."

Be ready and willing to process discomfort and allow failure to be a part of the journey towards your personal victory. *Practice doing what is necessary to achieve your goals.*

When designing solutions and offers for your market, do so from your heart, so they are original. Look at the challenges you've overcome in your own life. How can these experiences lead to practical solutions for your clients?

The results can be in a variety of common formats (templates, e-books, audits, workshops, mastermind programs, etc.). But make sure they align with who you are. When created, you should feel inspired, abundant to share them with the world.

To create a one-of-a-kind solution, you need to dedicate your time, money and energy. There is no overnight success. Be bold to stand in your truth and explore creative ways to deliver the solutions.

Through the design process, you will face inner monsters in different forms. You'll need to develop a strong discipline to overcome failures, obstacles and unforeseen circumstances during the course; and learn to apply different tools and techniques to conquer "bad days."

Be a lifelong learner and continue to work on yourself. Ask questions and apply feedback from reputable sources to polish up your solutions.

Surround yourself with people who can expand your perspectives and push you to reach new heights of success.

Deliver with so much value for your clients you blow their minds.

Realise the value of self-coaching. It is non-negotiable if you want to be a thought leader, and rise to the top 1% in your industry.

Courageously invent new ways of working that are *simple.*

Willpower, determination and perseverance will carry you through challenging periods. Celebrate your wins often—big or small, they are milestones to greater victories.

This is the magic pill you've been waiting for.

FROM YOUR EXPERIENCE TO THE CUSTOMER EXPERIENCE

Now you may be thinking, "Okay, Jocelyn, this sounds great, but what if no one gets me or what I'm trying to do. What if there are no customers?"

When you offer your unique style, when you put yourself and your superpowers out there, you become a beacon. You'll naturally attract clients who want to work with you. And as they use your gifts, they will share the positive impact they feel with others, drawing in even more people to buy from you.

BUILD AN ALIGNED TEAM

To be successful in business, you can't do it alone. Period. You must absolutely surround yourself with a high-performing team. They can help you turbo-charge your business performance.

Of course, that involves first sitting down and thoughtfully creating a list of skills and responsibilities you need at your disposal. This way, you'll identify individuals who can complement each other and bring your business forward.

Once again, you need to make bold and brave choices. It really is a million-dollar decision when it comes to recruiting and building a team happy to work for and represent your company.

At the same time, mastering the art of giving and receiving feedback is essential to getting the most from your team. If this isn't a skill that comes naturally, invest in personal coaching so you can communicate effectively. There are no shortcuts.

The golden truth: by surrounding yourself with high-performing team members, your business is guaranteed to thrive and flourish quickly.

BE THE CEO

As a CEO, you will experience plenty of failures and discover new lessons throughout your business journey. You can only scale Mount Everest one step at a time.

Some days, things will not go your way. The hiccups are guaranteed. You might worry, but truth be told, that's an indulgent emotion that has no benefit whatsoever. When you notice you're entering this territory, shift your focus. If you need to, get help to move forward.

At the same time, don't be distracted by other people's success. Skip the hours spent scrolling through social media, comparing someone else's end to your beginning.

You are the CEO. You cannot afford to take your eyes off the prize.

The quickest way to get to your destination is to do the work and focus on your own plan.

Use your time wisely. Host powerful and purposeful meetings people enjoy being part of.

Adopt productivity habits and be a role model to your team members. Be an example to your clients.

Get things done and be 100% present on the task at hand. Unsubscribe and unfollow distractions.

Don't indulge in emotions such as over-thinking, procrastination and overwhelm. Be mindful of the self-sabotage demon when it raises its head. Banish it, in no uncertain terms. Treat imposter syndrome the same way. Remind yourself you are enough.

These are things we all struggle with. You can wallow in them or get coaching to make a success-generating mind shift if you can't do it on your own. Powerful leaders know when they need help, and they ask for it.

Likewise, seasoned CEOs take opportunities to rest, retreat and spend time with people who lift them up. Follow suit. Develop genuine and lasting relationships with others. You are not a robot. Social interaction is a way to recharge your work brain.

Switching off this way can be harder than you think. But you know what they say about all work and no play. This applies to the company culture you build as well. Grow one that people dream to work in.

Be a kind, tender-hearted and compassionate leader, while learning how to say "no" graciously. Always leave someone better off than you found them.

Anyone can be a CEO in title. But it's completely different to behave like one. Share visions and empower your team to bring them to life. Open your eyes to possibilities while evaluating your company's progress regularly.

Ask these three powerful questions all the time:

1. What worked well?
2. What didn't work well?
3. What could we do differently?

Being really raw and honest with the assessment will only heighten your future success and allow you to find possibilities that would otherwise remain hidden.

Once you do, it's time to *delegate authority*—facilitate your team to work at an optimal level. Along with their responsibilities, they share a corresponding amount of authority. When you give them the freedom to use that authority, you ensure tasks are completed efficiently and allow each individual to be accountable for their work.

Delegation is sharing responsibility, ownership and decision making. You spend less time and effort monitoring and micromanaging when your team members are capable, competent and empowered.

It is also a way to maintain clear *boundaries*. You cannot do everything on your own. If you try to, you create energy blocks, physical, emotional and mental limits from over-committing yourself. By delegating workload, you say "no" to working on weekends and pushing yourself beyond what is humanly possible.

Be a role model of work-life balance, knowing you can depend on your team. Just maintain your professionalism throughout your interactions, though. It's common for colleagues to become favourites and friends. But you are, first and foremost, their leader.

MONEY MATTERS AND MATTERS OF MONEY

Business by design is step one of unlocking unlimited abundance. Step two requires challenging your psyche. And how you think about money is one of the key differentiators between five-figure and seven-figure incomes.

Be ready to be vulnerable and transparent with yourself.

As you evolve as a CEO, your money beliefs and stories will start to impact every aspect of your business.

What is your experience with money? How would you rate your relationship with it on a scale of zero to ten, with ten being "I love money and money loves me"? Take notes on how you handle money. From saving to spending, to how you think about it.

DO YOUR MONEY BELIEFS EMPOWER OR DISEMPOWER YOU?

Our lives are conditioned from the ages of zero to six. Your beliefs about money stem from family members, teachers, friends and society. Over time, the stories you hear about their financial experiences will influence your own thinking and conduct.

As a financial adviser with over fifteen years of experience, I have seen how disempowering money beliefs lead to poor choices. For instance, if money has always been tight in your family, you may reject the opportunities to invest in yourself and your business. You may settle for doing things on your own rather than hiring an expert, thereby slowing your growth potential.

Unless you can increase your self-awareness and let go of restrictive behaviour, you'll find yourself in a rut you cannot get out of. Your financial situation will reach a limit when, in truth, there is no ceiling.

So, tell me, what do you think when someone says "money"? Is it:

- Money is hard to get
- I have to work long hours to make money
- Money doesn't grow on trees
- Rich people are corrupt
- Money is not important to me
- Money is the root of evil

Now tell me: how do you describe yourself? For example, do you see yourself as a hard worker? Do you consider yourself a person of integrity, unfouled by the negative influence of money?

149

Take a moment to compare these two sets of thoughts. *You may begin to realise how much your fiscal beliefs impact the way you live.* Do you work long hours because you think that's the only way to deserve more? Do you stop yourself from increasing your prices because doing so would suggest you're money hungry?

As you build your awareness, pay attention to the corresponding emotions. Does thinking of money stress you out, fill you with worry and fear? Or does it make you feel abundant and expansive?

Disempowering beliefs usually bring about negative emotions, leading to self-sabotage, limiting behaviours and avoidance. *To desire money is not greed. It is a wish for security, independence, and recognition of the value you offer.*

Every negative money thought, if not addressed, will eventually hurt your business. If you want to build an unlimitedly abundant empire, a strong foundation of beliefs is a must.

When you have empowering money thoughts as a CEO, you will make million-dollar decisions like hiring the right and best people in the market and investing in systems to scale your operations. You will also invest in your personal development as a leader and make decisions that add value to your company.

Conversely, disempowering thoughts will trap you in a pattern of counting pennies, with no real financial growth.

There is plenty of money circulating around the world. And you deserve to have it come your way, as long as you serve others by creating valuable offers using your talents and skills.

UNLIMITED ABUNDANCE IN YOUR POCKET

So, where does this leave you?

If nothing else, I want you to recognise the wealth of your experiences. Be aware of how they've shaped you, how they can uplift or restrict your potential. Use them wisely by understanding their impact on your thoughts and actions, while also applying them to create unique avenues of business.

Developing your enterprise will get you far, but developing yourself will get you further. Believe me, you are worth the investment of self-discovery and self-improvement. Unlimited abundance follows soon after.

ABOUT THE AUTHOR

Jocelyn Chong is an award-winning, #1 International Best-Selling Author, CEO and Founder of Seed to Sequoia. After a successful twenty-year career in Banking and Finance, where she generated over $200 million in revenue, she changed paths to pursue her true passion as a Certified Life and Business Coach.

Utilizing her MBA and background in high-level sales, leadership and management, she has to date worked with over 500 entrepreneurs, teaching them how to earn with ease, attract dream clients, and create a life by design. Her mission is to help business leaders tap into their true purpose while scaling their business with feel-good strategies and intuitive guidance.

Jocelyn has been featured in Thrive Global, Digital Journal, FOX, Ask.com, The Times and Finance News World.

Her question for you is "HOW UNLIMITED DO YOU WANT TO BE?"

Website: *www.jocelynchong.com.au*
Instagram: *www.instagram.com/_jocelynchong_*
LinkedIn: *www.linkedin.com/in/jocelynchong*
Facebook: *www.facebook.com/jocelyn.chong.9674*

16

JOLYNN VAN ASTEN

IMAGINE THIS: THE WHOLE WORLD'S IN YOUR HANDS

"The moment you doubt whether you can fly, you cease forever to be able to do it."
- J. M. Barrie, Peter Pan

Hello, my friend. I am so grateful that you are here. You are a part of my dream fulfilled. Yes, you. Once upon a time, I imagined you were reading a chapter from a book that was published during a time when the world was changing so quickly, that every day felt as though 1,000 days had passed from dawn to dusk.

And here you are. We "dreamed" each other in. Whether consciously or unconsciously, you at some point knew, deep in your heart, that you would be called up to and for something greater. You knew that you would have an important role in a new era.

Now, that role may not be one that all beings on planet earth are aware of via media outlets, glossy magazine covers, or even podcast episodes. But oh, those beings who prayed to find you, who imagined in their hearts that there was someone who would understand them, who would "get them", right where they are on their journey, those beings know how important your role is.

So come on in, have a seat, and let's have a conversation about what I believe your greatest tools will be as you embark on your journey across uncharted territory.

Imagine you are here with me, on my sofa. Notice how welcoming the room is, the walls are crisp white, the rug is a blue-and-gold marble. If you slide your shoes off, you'll notice how soft and well-padded it is. There's a scent of fresh-cut flowers in the air, and the tea kettle is whistling with excitement that we are finally together.

There's a wind chime on my porch, and the patio door is open just enough that a gentle breeze is floating in carrying its soft sounds to you. As you glance toward the patio door, you notice a hummingbird feeder, and the little birds buzzing in and out, drinking, then rushing away. They aren't concerned with what we are talking about today, or are they?

I'll get your tea, have a seat and move the pillows just the way you like them. Let's talk about your role and the assets that will support you.

Have you imagined what your role in the Golden Age might be? Have you spent nights trying to fall asleep wondering what's next for you to do? Or do you know... do you already know deep in your heart what it is you're here to do?

More importantly, have you considered how you want to "be?" Because you're reading this, I believe you are wise and understand that your state of Being will permeate whatever you are doing.

Between us, there are two truly powerful assets required to have on this journey moving into this new Golden Age, (1) Your brilliant imagination, and (2) The ability to BE you.

Let's explore this further.

"Everything you can imagine is real."
- Pablo Picasso

IMAGINATION

Imagination is spoken about amongst the dreamers, the innovators, the change-makers. Personal development circles and your favorite yoga teacher probably fling the term around loosely. But today we're going to just talk about *yours*.

Your powerful imagination is required to create what you want in this world personally, as well as what you want to bring in for the greater good.

My hope is that you have been using your imagination as a powerful tool. Maybe you've tapped into its power from time to time and realized that you have been creating experiences in your reality. Maybe you've been a fan of great spiritual teachers who speak about it, maybe it's something you're learning how to operate intentionally.

Whatever your experience has been up until now is absolutely perfect.

I believe imagination is a higher faculty of the intellect. One definition of intellect is "mental powers of a particular person."

Imagination is truly a mental power that can be intentionally harnessed to create good in your life, and the lives of others. Consider people you know who tend to worry. How do they know what to worry about? It is all based on the images they are "imagining" within their inner reality. Those images either represent past experiences or they are vain imaginations of a future scene that has never happened. Most likely they are imagining an experience from the past and distorting it into a future scene. That is a powerful skill. Now, if that same skill was employed to create images of events turning out successfully, the person would literally experience deeper peace, and project that peace out into the future, the eternal now.

You can do this too. You can cultivate your imagination and help shape a global reality that allows humankind to live in a world of peace, joy, love and personal growth.

"Imagine all the people livin' life in peace."
- John Lennon

WHO YOU BE

Yes, "who you be." You beyond your ego/personality is who is required to show up and fulfill your new role. The "you" who got you to the point in your life up until now will need to shift again. S/he will be required to be an updated version of her/himself. Keeping all the wisdom you've acquired up until now, as well as releasing patterns and attitudes that keep you limited in any way.

"When you see a thing clearly in your mind, your creative "success mechanism" within you takes over and does the job much better than you could do it by conscious effort or "willpower."
- Maxwell Maltz

Guess what? Your imagination asset will be able to be employed to release YOU. How? By imagining the YOU that you are without certain patterns and attitudes, and imagining you operating in this world at your true divinely given capacity. The truth is, as discussed in the seminal work of Dr. Maxwell Maltz, *Psycho-Cybernetics*, you can't outperform your own self-image. Even if that self-image is unconsciously operating, it will limit your capabilities to fulfill your role.

Your conscious awareness of where you are heading in your new role can shift quickly by expanding your conscious awareness via your imagination.

How do you know what your conscious awareness is of your current self-image? It is a reflection of what is happening in your life right now. You can look around your surroundings, who you hang out with, what you do for a living and notice that it all reflects your current unconscious self-image. No judgment, it isn't good or bad, it just is. However, it is time to shift again.

I encourage you to start to daydream again about what's possible as we collectively move into this new age. There will be certain states of being that you need to cultivate practicing living in there will be new perceptions and attitudes to take on. New dreams to engage with. And wisdom tools that you'll be needing to impart to others.

Because you will be in a role that requires you to walk your talk, to shine light, and to be a true living example of what is possible for others. Now, this can seem like a daunting task; however, it's actually a natural assignment. Because you already are and you already possess everything you need to move forward and be you.

"A man's chief delusion is his conviction that there are causes other than his own state of consciousness. All that befalls a man—all that is done by him, all that comes from him—happens as a result of his state of consciousness. A man's consciousness is all that he thinks and desires and loves, all that he believes is true and consents to. That is why a change of consciousness is necessary before you can change your outer world. Rain falls as a result of a change in the temperature in the higher regions of the atmosphere, so, in like manner, a change of circumstance happens as a result of a change in your state of consciousness."
- Neville Goddard, The Power of Awareness

STATES OF BEING

We, as humans, are thinking/feeling systems. I believe our emotions follow our thoughts. A state is literally an activated biochemical neural network which contains emotional components and internal images. It's ambiguous. You can experience any state now just by shifting your attention and accessing a state that you desire. This is great news, because as you engage with your new self image you use your imagination to release, you'll be able to access states of being like joy, boldness, clarity, peace, tenacity and more on command.

By living in the state of being you wish to experience now, you will not only release ways of being that you don't want to take forward with you. You will also embody states that you do!

"Man maintains his balance, poise, and sense of security only as he is moving forward."
- Maxwell Maltz

Imagining your new role and self-image of you living in that role may be easier than you think. Let's engage in a brief exercise. Yes, feel free to write in this book if it is in print form, or get a notepad or tablet to write on if you have the digital or audio version.

1. What are you imagining life to be like in the future for yourself?
2. What are you imagining you doing?
3. What are you wearing?
4. Who are you with?
5. What are you imagining the global vibration to be like in the collective human experience?
6. What are you imagining technology to do for us?
7. What are you imagining people will say about what you're up to in the world?
8. What is your deepest heart's desire for humanity?
9. What might you hear a small child of the future say to you in conversation?
10. What attitude did you release?
11. What attitude did you embrace?
12. What toxic habits did you release freely?
13. What healthy habits did you willingly embrace?

These imagination starters are just the beginning. I encourage you to carve out time each day to imagine your life on this planet, moving forward. Give yourself the space to see with your inner vision the way you want things to be. Train yourself to drop your focus off of what you do not want to see, be, or experience. Train yourself to only focus on what you truly want. Since 2020, we have all been embracing uncertainty in new ways. I invite you to activate the mighty power of your imagination and use it for good. Good for you, your loved ones, and good for humanity.

You truly do have the whole world in your hands.

Please enjoy the upcoming coloring page illustrated by Jolynn Van Asten. Consider using it as a meditation tool. Simply take a few deep breaths, consider how you want to be in the Golden Age, and contemplate those thoughts while you add color to the drawing.

ABOUT THE AUTHOR

Jolynn Van Asten is the founder of Experience 144™, a well-being company.

She is a certified trainer of Brain-Based Leadership and Intuitive Expressive Art. She holds additional certifications and degrees in Humanistic Neuro-Linguistic Psychology (HNLP), neuroplasticity coaching, Mindfulness Meditation, and Holistic Life Counseling.

She is the co-author and illustrator of the *I Am a Difference Maker* children's creativity book and the author of the forthcoming children's book, *The Dream Of The Little Buffalo*, which tells the tale of how creativity can eradicate the effects of human suffering.

She runs certification programs in Intuitive Expressive Arts and works with clients privately who seek Intuitive Expressive Art Experiences for transformation and greater well-being.

Website: *www.experience144.com*
Email: *vip@experience144.com*

17

KA KI LEE

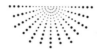

THE NICE, GOOD GIRL

I was brought up a nice, good girl.

What is nice?

What is good?

It depends on how you look at it. The dictionary says that 'nice' is to give pleasure or satisfaction while 'good' is to be desired or approved of, of high quality, possessing or displaying moral virtue, giving pleasure, thorough, valid.

But who decides what is nice and what is good?

I do.

It was me using what I thought was the gold standard—other people's definition.

I ticked all the 'nice' and 'good' boxes with a cherry on top.

I followed the rules, I didn't speak up, I got things done, I fitted in, I aimed to please everyone but myself—I was nice, I was good.

From an early age, people told me I was nice, good, smart, wise, mature, pretty, confident and myriads of other positive traits. I remember a time that I believed it all but I'm not sure what happened, and I can't even pinpoint when it started, but one by one, I stopped believing that I was any of those things, because...

I was the nice, good girl who went with whatever my parents said. I was told to choose a profession that is reputable and makes money so I can buy a house, pay off the mortgage and work until I retire. Pharmacy is a great profession for a girl because you don't need to be on call, you get paid well and working hours are more flexible because, you know, children. So, from the age of twelve, I said I wanted to be a pharmacist or doctor, not really knowing what it all meant and guess what? I became a pharmacist.

I did not make my own decisions.

I was the nice, good girl who decided to rebel when I was sixteen. I met a boy. I was controlled by the boy. I was cheated on by the boy. I found my voice and lost my voice speaking up against him. I broke my parents' hearts, I broke friendships and worst of all I broke myself because little did anyone know that I was physically, verbally, and emotionally abused. I knew the relationship wasn't good for me from the beginning, but my stubbornness made me stay, my need to rebel made me stay, my hurt ego made me stay, and being made to believe I wasn't good enough made me stay—all these things made me stay for three years.

I did not respect myself.

I was the nice, good girl who was trying to get off the lap of an "uncle" who was supervising his son and my brother playing in his son's room. He wouldn't let me off his lap no matter how hard I fought and he touched me inappropriately. I was scared. I remember telling my parents, but what does an eight-year-old know. Or maybe I was nine. It didn't matter, it happened, and it happened one too many times. I managed to suppress these memories for the next twenty years.

I was not heard. I was not seen.

I was the nice, good girl who dropped everything to make sure my friends were looked after. Puking in the toilet, I'm there to wipe your spew. Boyfriend problems, I'm there to listen and support. Need a vent, my ears are yours. Husband missing while you're in labour, no problem, I'm there to cut the umbilical cord. It didn't matter if I was busy, didn't really want to wipe up spew or had other things going on. I looked after everyone, but no one looked after me. I never asked for help, and no one ever asked if I needed help either because I always had it together.

I was co-dependent.

I was the nice, good girl who poured my heart and soul into work to make sure that systems were fixed, and my staff were looked after, that they were seen, heard, and held. Just pregnant, suddenly taking on the role of Chief Pharmacist when all I wanted to do was be horizontal and not throw up. Working twelve to thirteen hour days, being paid less per hour than my assistant, wanting to please, wanting to serve, wanting to be liked, wanting to make things better for everyone, dealing with sides of colleagues I had never experienced before, not receiving support from my managers and all the while being scared of doing it all wrong.

I was not sure of myself.

I was the nice, good girl who didn't tell my husband how much I resented him for not being there for me. For getting me pregnant then leaving me for weeks at a time, for leaving me to single parent for weeks at a time, for getting me pregnant again and leaving me for weeks at a time, for having a career, for having sleep, for not doing the housework and for not having to think about all the things that need to be done because I feared I'll lose him. So, I just got on with it.

I was exhausted.

I was the nice, good girl who didn't understand why my business wasn't working even though I was doing the "work." Everything I touch always works—it was a given and it was always easy. Good grades, fixing broken systems, implementing changes, building relationships, learning new things, making money, you name it... I was able to do it with ease, grace, and flow. It didn't make sense to me, I felt broken, dumb, stupid for even thinking of starting my own business. I should just keep working because then I have something to show but I also knew that I was meant for more. I wished that voice inside my head telling me I was meant for more would go away. What was wrong with me? What does more even mean?

I was lost.

I was the nice, good girl who refused to admit that I had post-natal depression because I'm not someone who would get post-natal depression. I walked around like nothing was wrong, hiding behind my mask of positivity, niceness, and goodness. I couldn't understand why I felt so sad when my life was perfect on the outside—amazing husband, beautiful child, multiple properties, investments, reputable profession, multiple six-figure incomes… I checked all the success boxes, but why was I crying every night? What was missing?

It was Me.

I was missing.

I needed MY support.

I needed MY cup filled.

I needed MY love.

I needed MY trust.

I needed MY heart to open.

I needed to listen to MY soul.

I needed to find Me.

These realisations didn't come to me overnight. There was a lot of crying, questioning, learning, and healing that happened before the dots connected.

It was messy, it was ugly, it was perfect.

I am the nice, good girl who wrestled with my ego and to some extent my parents' ego to let go of a career in a reputable profession. I realised that my job title does not define me and that four years in University can't determine what I do for the rest of my life. I went from pharmacist to trading on the stock market, coaching, healing, and podcasting. I know if I wanted to do something else, I can, and it doesn't make me less or more of a person. It is who I am. I no longer wanted to put myself in a box and I know following what lights me up is my way.

I am decisive.

I am the nice, good girl who refused to be in another relationship unless I was treated with respect. I had to heal from the trauma and open my heart to trust and allow another person in. I did, and he is one of the best decisions of my life. We are a team - we communicate deeply, we love deeply, and we respect and support each other deeply. Many of my friends comment on how lucky I am to have such a great relationship—it's not luck, it's both inner work and teamwork.

I am self-respect.

I am the nice, good girl who suddenly remembered the trauma of being sexually abused by that "uncle" on a yoga trip with my girlfriends in Bali. The flood gates opened. I went home and told my husband, but I needed another ten years before I was able to speak to my parents about it. The moment I told them, I was heard and seen by them, and it was the greatest healing and release.

I am heard. I am seen.

I am the nice, good girl who realised I was co-dependent and needed boundaries. So, I distanced myself from people that sucked my energy and put up an energetic barrier to make sure I don't absorb the negativity. I stopped trying to fix everyone. I am there for my friends, only if my cup is full. I stopped being in other people's business because it was none of my business. My relationships changed for the better and I feel better.

I am interdependent.

I am the nice, good girl who continued to pour my heart and soul into work to make sure that systems were fixed, and my staff were looked after, that they were seen, heard, and held. Being a workaholic, I still worked more than I was paid for, but I no longer needed to please or needed to be liked. I knew who I was, and I asked for support when I needed it. I wasn't afraid to do things wrong and if I was wrong, I wasn't afraid to admit either. I was more vulnerable than ever, and it was perfect. I respected myself, I respected my staff, I love everyone I worked with, and I was there to serve as a leader. I didn't let myself down.

I am sure of myself.

I am the nice, good girl who tells my husband exactly how I feel. If he is annoying me, I'll tell him. If I'm upset at him even though it's not his fault, I tell him. If I'm feeling loved up because he really is the best husband in the whole wide world, I tell him. If I need help, I tell him because he deserves to know what I'm thinking rather than guessing or just plain not knowing. I let go of my resentment because he didn't know how I felt or the reasons why but I had expected him to know. Communication is key in any relationship. It really is.

I am at peace.

I am the nice, good girl who finally understood why my business wasn't working and it wasn't because I was broken, dumb or stupid. It was because I was out of alignment, doing something that wasn't lighting me up, that didn't align with my values and where I had to push. I realised all the times when things worked with ease, grace and flow were when I was doing things that lit me up, aligned with my values, and I did not push and allowed it to flow.

I am clarity.

I am the nice, good girl who awakened to discover that the real reason I was depressed was because I was not living in alignment with my soul. I created success using other people's measures of success. I believed what I was told to believe. I did what other people told me were nice and good to do. I didn't listen to my intuition. I didn't trust myself. I didn't surrender. I didn't allow. I didn't have faith. I didn't think for myself. I didn't know myself. These most glorious realisations allowed me to change every aspect of my life. It is with this awareness that I continue to evolve and live more in alignment with my soul.

I am Me

I am no longer missing.

I am supporting Me.

I am filling MY cup.

I love Me.

I trust Me.

I am opening MY heart.

I am listening to MY soul.

I found Me.

～

These are but a snapshot of the many stories that make up my journey so far. Although my journey is uniquely mine, the stories are not.

I have met many souls who share one or more of my stories. Our stories. Some are nice, good girls just like me, while others are not. Does it matter?

No.

All of us share the need for self-love, self-respect, self-expression, self-worth, to be heard, to be seen, to be held and to feel love, joy and peace. That is what all souls want and that is my want for you.

Thirty-nine years Earthside and I feel that my life is just beginning. I am forever a work in progress.

Before I awakened, I believed there would be a time that I'll arrive. I'll arrive at the place, time, status that I believed would show my success in this life, but that illusion has been knocked out of me.

Know that, once you say yes to your personal and spiritual growth, you realise that you never arrive. There is no final destination, however, you will arrive at many landmarks and these landmarks serve as check-points along your journey. Some of these landmarks are breathtaking, some not so much but each of them is a reminder of how far you've come since the last one.

You are a beautiful piece of art that continues to evolve and grow. Wear every battle scar with pride, that is your success, you made it to the other side. You passed, you grew, and you can now pass your wisdom to those after you.

There are times that I fall back to my old patterns, I am not perfect, and I don't want to be. I recognise that it's just another layer of the same story I tell myself, disguised in a different form that needs to be released.

What has helped me immensely is self-awareness.

Self-awareness is the first step to healing because without it, you don't know what needs to heal. All the stories you tell yourself without your awareness because it's part of your normal self-dialogue.

I'm not good enough.

I'm not pretty enough.

I'm not skinny enough.

I'm not smart enough.

I'm not worthy enough.

I'm not enough.

The problem is the stories you tell yourself can be misleading. On the surface, the stories may seem harmless and sometimes it may even be beautifully wrapped with a big sparkly bow but once you are aware and pull off the bow and unwrap it, you'll find that these harmless stories are an "I'm not enough" story.

When you tell yourself you are not enough, you are also telling yourself that you are not deserving and when you tell yourself you are not deserving, you are telling yourself you do not love yourself.

Self-love, I truly believe, is where everything stems from..

Every snapshot of my journey, I healed myself with an act of self-love. Every act of self-love helped me to heal and with healing, it helped me change my life and heal those around me.

It's a ripple of love and it's a ripple that I never want to end.

Take time to build your self-awareness muscle, spend a week taking note of all your fleeting thoughts and write down as many as you can. What stories are you telling yourself? How often are you telling yourself these stories?

Remember there is nothing wrong with you.

Stop beating yourself up.

When you're ready to release those stories, you do not need to do it alone. There are people before you who have gone through the same and they are there to help you.

Find someone that feels right. Don't just go by credentials.

Trust your intuition.

It is time that you do.

You do not need to change who you are. You need to find who you are.

Know that, I am still nice. I am still good.

The difference now is that I no longer define nice and good by how I think others define it but by how my soul defines it.

I am a nice, good girl.

ABOUT THE AUTHOR

Ka Ki Lee is a multi-passionate entrepreneur. Her main endeavours include being a mother of two, an Unhustle For Abundance Coach and Healer, Founder and Creator of Unlimited Abundance Academy, Share Trader and Host of The Awakened Feminine podcast. After spending over twenty years in the healthcare industry as a Hospital Pharmacist, Ka Ki took a leap of faith and left corporate to begin her entrepreneurial journey. With a background rooted in science, she combines both a logical and intuitive approach to help her clients release the limiting beliefs, blocks and programming that are stopping them from living the life of wealth and abundance they deserve.

Her two biggest passions right now are to help busy entrepreneurs and professionals create money on the US stock market in under one hour per week using the strategy that replaced her six-figure income, allowing her to quit her career as a Hospital Pharmacist and to use her podcast as a platform for thought leaders from around the world to share the love and wisdom they've collected along their life journey—their stories, lessons, tips and expertise in their field – to inspire people to live a soul-aligned life.

Website: www.kakilee.com
Facebook: www.facebook.com/abundancewithkakilee
Instagram: www.instagram.com/abundancewithkakilee
and www.instagram.com/theawakenedfemininepodcast
LinkedIn: www.linkedin.com/in/kakilee

OLIVE MACDONAGH

CLEARING THE SHITE TO FIND THE LIGHT!

Let food be our medicine, let nature be our guide
Let sound be the healing force that takes us deep inside
Let us raise the Kundalini, set our gifts alight
Let us shine our lights together, we're alive!

Every day seemed like a month. Each dragged on, moment by moment, counting down the hours 'til the end of each week. I felt like the weight of the world was upon my shoulders from the mix of deadline pressures and absolute boredom, meaninglessness and monotony of it all. Regurgitating the same tasks over and over with as much joy as tearing out my own hair. Any flicker of joy inside me was dwindling to a kindle from what I felt I was doing, or more so not doing with my own life.

You see, I "should" have been delighted with my life. A sponsorship from school into a 'big four' accountancy firm and making my way to "Success." Was a promotion to Associate Director in a multi-national firm not enough to keep me happy? Leaving my home in Ireland to work in the Caribbean with tax-free pay? The sun, the sea and sand with a top-notch view from my balcony? Surely, I had "made it"? I had even hit the ultimate "six-figure income" that I thought I always wanted. This was it, right?

Well, it didn't feel that way. My head sometimes thought that it was, but my heart definitely didn't feel it. I had buried my feelings deep inside as I churned out those accounts and made the best of it. I felt stuck in someone else's version of what life should be like, but it definitely wasn't mine. My dad was an accountant, my older sister was an accountant, and my older brother was an accountant. Sure, what else would I be???!!! I didn't know how to ask for what I wanted and especially when an opportunity was paid for and on a platter. It was a no-brainer...emmmm more like a no-hearter!

In each position, I slowly navigated my way into a training role to make it seem more human and ensured that I was on the social committee and got involved in every sports team going to make life more enjoyable at the office. Outside the office, I really enjoyed singing in a choir and had a few other activity outlets for my own sanity! Don't get me wrong, it wasn't all bad, and I did have plenty of 'fun' at the weekends and holidays, but I was slowly dying inside. I knew deep within me that there had to be more to life than this nine-to-five gig that I had allowed my life to become. I needed more, but I didn't know what to do about it. Would everyone "approve" if I left?

...And how would I support myself if I left the rat race? I was used to my comforts, after all!

I struggled in the environment, with all the computer vibes, and could actually feel that having so much technology around me was affecting me. I could feel my body repelled by the vibrations as I became more sensitive. I remember days that I actually felt physically sick at the thought of going to work. Towards the end of my career, I consciously witnessed the apparent lunacy of so many people spending most of their waking hours in an office. Our one life in what can seem like a cold, cut-throat and institutionalised environment, bad for our health and happiness. This job was not meeting any of my top values, but back then I hadn't even taken the time to discover my own values, so I hadn't realised it consciously. It felt like I was selling my soul. NO MONEY WAS WORTH THIS.

In the earlier years, to escape my office reality, I would go out partying at the weekends to make up for my terrible week. I'd go binge drinking "for the craic" as we like to call it in Ireland. I would inhale bottles of red wine and could easily go through more than a packet of cigarettes on a night out. *Fags*, as we used to call them in Ireland. I'd spend a fortune on clothes, shoes, handbags, make-up, hair, jewellery and all the regalia to have myself ready for the incessant gallivanting. I'd stay up half way through the night dancing and back to a house party after so as not to miss out on any devilment! I loved to dance, and the music was *doof-doof-doof* galore. I wonder, if I had enjoyed my working life, would I have reached for all these unhealthy substances that were to take their toll on my body? I certainly have no desire to now!

With a hangover, I would then eat crap, and I gorged into junk food with cravings galore for a few days after. This would then be a double whammy and exacerbate health issues to come. This was all bound to take its toll eventually, but back then, it seemed like the norm, quite bizarrely. Any night I was absolutely wrecked, it wasn't long before I'd hit the "shots" or vodka red bull for a fix, and sometimes, something even stronger if it was easily available. Anything that was going, I was game to try, "for tricks" as I like to say. I love to experience all that life has to offer, but ideally, I would have been a bit better at setting healthy boundaries for myself. An emerging theme to explore in my life!

If that wasn't enough action, I played competitive sports too. I trained hard, played hard and captained some teams in Gaelic and Rugby when I lived in The Cayman Islands and when I first moved back to Ireland. I loved that go-go-go energy because it made me feel really alive, and I just loved the social aspect of it too. Talk about working hard and playing hard. It was bound to end sooner or later. Now when I look back at it all, I was on a treadmill and going ninety!

In 2008 I had moved back home temporarily to Ireland due to family circumstances calling me and one day in the office, I noticed my abdomen really swollen, so much so that I couldn't close my pants. My nice boss at the time sent me off to the doctor, and I was rushed into hospital for emergency surgery. Stage IV endometriosis was revealed as the cause of a cyst that they feared had ruptured and was removed, thankfully, leaving me to rest and re-evaluate my life. In the previous years, I had started to become very unwell, and no one knew what was wrong. I was in and out of doctors' and hospitals and being told it was all "in my head" because my illness was invisible and they couldn't find a label for what I was going through. I knew deep inside that it was related to my working in a job that was not aligned with me, but try explaining that to a family of accountants... good luck! I *should* have been grateful for all I had. I *should* have wanted to keep the safety of my stable income...*shouldn't I?*

The doctors gave me six weeks to rest. For the first time, I had that time to ponder what the hell I was gonna do with my life. Being single at the time, my mum offered for me to stay in her house to rest and recover. This was my opportunity to start my research and ultimately led me to my journey to health and going within. I knew that I had to take responsibility for my own life and in particular, my health and wellbeing. I had to take the first steps, no matter how small, for anything to change. Once I was well enough to travel, I booked a nutrition and relaxation retreat. I had no idea it was going to change my life so much. It was a miracle. It opened a whole new world that I never knew existed. I was blown away by the absolute acceptance. I was inspired by the energy of a place that completely welcomed me wherever I was at. I was reconnected to parts of myself that I had never felt before, or if I had, I couldn't remember. Walking around that place, in that moment, I knew what I wanted my life to become. I wanted to live in a place like this and help people like this. Inspiration hit. "I will create somewhere like this for people to come and enjoy someday!" Most importantly, I gave myself permission.

After my six weeks, I went back to work reluctantly but with a different perspective and a deep knowing and wish that someday my life would be different. I felt even more distant from this career that was doing nothing for my health and wellness. I had changed inside and even though the outside looked the same, I wasn't!

I had to make a plan, but it seemed like I had no choice about anything yet, as I still felt stuck and obliged to everyone else's plans for me. I had given my power away to external circumstances and thought that I *had to* do this, that and the other. I made a pact with myself and promised myself that if I ended up having a second surgery that I would definitely leave my job as then I would KNOW that my job was the reason that I was sick.

Surgery two came and went, and I still didn't feel strong enough as I was so afraid of all the judgement, and I hadn't tapped into my personal power or trust to move forward with my vision. After surgery three and a reduction in my health and quality of life that couldn't be ignored, it was just a matter of time before I built up the courage and felt comfortable enough to take the risk. My mind had started to develop a keen interest in nutrition as I delved into taking better care of myself, and by then, I was thinking that training as a nutritionist could be my first step.

My heart, on the other hand, was getting more upset. I remember standing in the shower that monumental morning, tears streaming down my face uncontrollably before a day at work. That sobbing and truly feeling my feelings was a game-changer. I didn't want to live this life anymore. I wasn't suicidal but had opened a door of major clarity. I did not want to continue the life that I was living. In that moment I knew that things HAD to change. I would, instead of killing myself or dying, just simply start to create a new life for myself.

I remember feeling a mix of nervousness and excitement and nearly like something much bigger than me helped me to stand up and walk from my desk into the HR office to hand in my notice. I didn't really know what would happen, but I felt an urge so great that I knew, no matter what, I wanted to leave my old life behind and start a new one. I was prepared to deal with the consequences, whatever they might be. Some deep part of me had to trust that I would be taken care of by the universe and that everything, no matter what, would be OK.

SO WHAT NOW? I began my soul searching after that pivotal moment and decided that it was time to explore my passions and unleash my gifts to serve the world. I would open a retreat! My family thought that I had lost the plot. Left a career with a stable income to invite strangers into my home to do woo -woo stuff. WTF?

You'd swear I was going to the top of a mountain to sell feathers. No one around me could comprehend what I was doing. Was I going mad? Maybe all the hormonal drugs that I was being fed before I came off all medication had taken its toll on my mental clarity, hey?

Where to start... my passion for nutrition! I wanted to share with people how to improve health naturally with juices and nature's nutrition now that I was feeling so much better with what I had implemented. That would definitely be part of my offering. I had also been giving Reiki treatments and enjoying that, so I would bring that in to my retreats too. Clients would love some yoga and meditation, so I would also train in that. I was finding Kundalini Yoga amazing for my own recovery. I realised that I could do whatever I wanted and it felt so freeing. AT LAST!

My strength was a huge asset that I had enjoyed before I got sick. I needed to learn how to channel any strength to bring about the change that I actually wanted. I had a pattern of doing WAY too much, so I had to learn how to slow down and put my strength and focus into self-care. After I became ill, my strength disappeared for a while, and I felt like I was so old for a few years. I felt totally disconnected from life-force and my homeopath recommended Kundalini Yoga to help me with that. This became a transformative tool that I ended up training in and remains so valuable in the work that I share in bringing people back into their power and back into their hearts.

I also had an insight in meditation that unless singing was part of my work, it would never be enough to satisfy me. Shortly enough thereafter, I realised that I could play live music and sing as part of my yoga and meditation experience and play sound healing instruments as part of my sound healing sessions. Mantra music is something that brings me the most connection of all and sound is a healing force that brings me so deep inside that I have connected with channelling transformative vibrations and healing. It's so interesting that things that seem obvious after they happen can be there staring at us, but we can't see them until we clear the shite that's stopping us see the light!

The last piece of the retreat puzzle for me was helping people to clear all the emotional shite with a tool that I could talk to clients with. I found the most amazing tool to help with this, which I use with my energy work here called Emotional Freedom Technique. Check out my blog on this if you haven't heard about it before!

This first big step had set the energy in motion for my retreat, a dream come true. An action with a rippling butterfly effect so large that it was the seed of what's now a place where I can connect deeply within myself and with others. One of the best things I have ever done. If I had known the joy that I would receive from each morning being able to leisurely stroll around my garden and pick my homegrown fresh fruit and veg in awe and bliss, I may have done it sooner but I trust that everything was in its divine timing. A couple of relapses into the accountancy world as I got my shit together. I am so glad now. I finally took the courage to take a risk and "let go" of my old life. As they say, no risk, no reward!

I now live in a place where I share my voice and healing music, a place where I feel the juicy life of freedom that I'd always wanted. A space where I and my guests can explore our gifts and where we chant, move, meditate, juice, cook, chat and wander in the gorgeous garden together. A space where we "clear the shite to find the light!" as I like to call it. Letting go of things that in our hearts we know are holding us back from living our dreams is a way to let LIGHT in. Ask yourself now: "What do I need to 'let go' of to get closer to my dreams?"

It's miraculous when we show up for ourselves like that and it ripples profound change in our lives on so many levels and in the lives of those around us. A small simple step on a journey of becoming who we're meant to be, truly living our purpose on this earth.

My health journey is a story that involves many chapters of practical and "woo-woo" adventures. A spontaneous Kundalini awakening type experience during a guided meditation, following my dreams to sing and record my own mantra music. Dietary changes, yoga and meditation, sound and energy healing and much self-exploration. Simple but not all easy... yet SO worth it! Transforming from a binge drinking, rugby playing, chartered accountant to a juice-drinking sound and energy healing yogini who chants as she plants... and LOVING IT! I never regret taking that bold step that opened a whole new world.

I hope that this inspires you to take YOUR first step in letting go of whatever is holding you back from your dream being expressed in this world. No one can take that step for you! Know that only YOUR step can bring whatever YOUR dream is to life. If you'd like to take some time out to reflect and discover what your dream is, or power up your courage to take that first step, I'd love to meet you here. My dream was and is a health and wellness retreat in the heart of Ireland where people feel inspired to unleash their gifts and create the life that they've always dreamed of. Thankfully, it's real now. Wanna come visit or connect online and be part of my dream? I hope so!

ABOUT THE AUTHOR

Olive MacDonagh is the founder of Butterfly Cottage Retreat in the heart of Ireland. She is a sound healer and energy therapist, holistic nutritionist, kundalini yoga & meditation teacher, mantra artist and hostess of the mostess! She deeply relaxes and nourishes guests with delights for all of the senses and woos with her deliciously fresh juices, raw healthy chocolate, healing sounds and angelic voice.

Olive is a nature lover with a passion for growing and foraging food in her beautiful garden. She has created wonderful online courses, notebook journals and relaxing mantra music and has

featured in Positive Life Magazine, Women's Way Magazine and the Elaine show as a recommended place to visit for a health boost and some restorative time out. Sign up on her website for a free video series on how to make meditation easier and blogs sharing her healing music.

Website: *www.butterflycottageretreat.ie*
Email: *olive@butterflycottageretreat.ie*
Facebook: *www.facebook.com/butterflycottageretreat*

19

THERESE SKELLY

THE POWER OF LETTING GO

L ooking down at my now strangely deformed finger, I just knew. Something was very, very wrong. I'd been out walking the dog, stopped at the park, and decided to sit on the grass for a bit. Enjoying a beautiful sunny day in Scottsdale, Arizona, after eight months of having Covid damage to my lungs, I had only recently built back up enough stamina to start exercising. The prior week, I had finally returned to taking Pilates classes, and each day I was feeling stronger in my body after what had been a horrible year.

While I sat there in a sweet, meditative state, my dog had other ideas. Out of the blue, Murphy, who had been lying behind me, went after somebody walking through the park. He's a big cattle dog and the force of his lunging caused the leash to be ripped out of my hand. After I got the dog back, I knew a trip to the ER was needed.

X-rays showed that my ring finger was badly broken and would need surgery. Additionally, the other fingers were sprained and to top it off... it was my dominant hand.

This crazy dog accident really took me down, because the previous year, I injured my wrist in a bicycle accident and was pretty much out of commission. After wearing splints and doing therapy for 4 months, I had just gone back to Pilates for a week, and then Covid hit! And it hit me hard.

So after two injuries in a year, when the "dog incident" happened, I had an absolutely "WTF" moment!

When I went to the hand surgeon who told me I would need surgery (with screws to hold the bone in place, I was crushed. After months of dealing with Covid, I'd finally gotten healthy and bam...it was taken away. I kept asking, "What was in my consciousness that was attracting injury to myself."

Did I feel like a victim? Oh, heck yeah. I wondered if indeed I was cursed, or so horribly damaged that I was unconsciously sabotaging myself over and over. Maybe you have felt this way if things haven't worked out for you.

But this isn't a story about my dog. This is about the stuff that happens in our lives, the story of how very often, just when we think we are ready to be productive and create new things, life throws us situations that force a hard stop. Why? Perhaps because we need to let go and "be" on this journey to empowerment.

Thanks to my years of spiritual practice, I managed to get myself to the point of understanding that this was happening for me, and not to me. I knew that there had to be some Divine Order in there somewhere. And I knew that if I kept digging and opening myself up to it, I'd find the answers.

So when I began reflecting, I saw for years that life was showing me something very different. For decades, my sense of self-worth was tied to what I could achieve, who I could help, and how much I could do. I had an identity of an alpha woman, being willing to hustle and get stuff done. I was often a leader in every organization I partnered with, and the person you could always count on to deliver.

Being stopped again with this new injury, what I found was the understanding that the little voice of Spirit inside me led me to the understanding that my "work" wasn't to be working in the physical. It wasn't time to focus on growing my business. No. My work was to learn to receive more, trust that I'd be taken care of, and to go even deeper in healing than I had ever done.

Perhaps you can relate. Have you ever had something that you wanted so badly, but for whatever reason, it didn't work? Or have you been working on a project, and it got stalled? Or maybe you experienced a loss, or death, or careened down a course that you didn't plan on.

Maybe, like me, you're drawn to all the things that this book promises, right? How to be... Uncensored. Untamed. Unleashed. Because leaders and highly driven women NEED to be all those things, right? But maybe, like me, you find, at times, that you're none of those things.

For instance, I grew up in a dysfunctional alcoholic home, and was extremely censored with the shame of my environment. I was trained not to talk about the craziness we were living and pretend that we were a functional, happy family. I learned how to shut down my knowing and stop listening to my inner awareness and truth.

I was *tamed* by the need to look good, be a people pleaser, and code-pendent caretaker. This led to perfectionism, lack of self-value, and a boatload of over giving to try to get my needs met. This pattern, by the way, is what so many of my beloved clients have gone through as well.

And I was very, very *leashed* to trauma that robbed me of my spirit. In fact, it has taken me decades of doing the work, so my nervous system is finally rewired to joy and hope as my set points.

Because of my history, the idea of being uncensored, untamed, and unleashed meant that I had to do things.

Unfortunately, I got wired to the identity that who I was is what I was overcoming, or the work I was doing. My value was dependent on what I could do and who I could support, fix, or save. Sadly, I think a lot of women's identities get tied up in this same dynamic. Our culture and upbringing teach this to us.

My quest for freedom always involved my DOING something. There was no stopping. And when I jumped into the entrepreneurial world, it was exacerbated. There is so much work in growing a business. Doing all that, and overcoming my trauma, challenges in relationships and having money issues, kept me on a constant merry-go-round of working on myself. I certainly don't regret any of that.

Becoming a business coach and helping people has been a huge blessing and is my life's work. I stepped into the role of a powerful mentor because of being on the journey myself, thus being able to hold space for my clients. But success in these areas solidified the "doing" as my identity got more and more wrapped around my six-figure business and what I was creating in the world.

Going through hand therapy has been eye opening. When I asked why my fingers were so stiff and swollen, the therapist explained the mechanism of scar tissue. She said that when there is an injury, the body protects it by surrounding it with scar tissue. On one hand, that's exquisite. The body knows just what to do to assist with healing and safety. But what if there have been emotional injuries? The "scar tissue" happening here often shows up as protective beliefs, ideas, or even personas. While they keep you safe, they keep you from truly living as well.

Here's an example: Let's say you come to me for mentoring, and I design some new programs with you. You're super excited to get this work out in the world because you know it's more in alignment with your soul's mission. You have a fabulous plan, yet you start hearing that little voice in your head. You know the one. It's the voice that tells you that you already charge a lot, and you can't raise your rates. Or reminds you that none of this is original and in fact Tony Robbins already said this, and everybody knows it anyway, so why bother. Or you have no room in your calendar, so just stick with what's already working and not expand into what you really want to do.

These are protective mechanisms. That means when you have had troubling experiences in your life, there is a part of you that will go out of its way to make sure you are not harmed again by attempting to have you stay the same. And 'the same' is often the things that got us validated, rewarded, or some brownie points for who we are "being."

And most of us have had those experiences. So, we find ourselves unconsciously holding ourselves back, or maybe we are running what I call "proving energy: having to be the best, over giving, or being everything to everybody. Not stopping or saying no." It's a lot of freaking work and truthfully, it can be exhausting. Many women entrepreneurs I know have suffered burned-out adrenals because of being on this quest to prove our value by showing how much we can get done and achieve.

That takes me to the process of deep learning from this broken hand. From being injured before, I know how to receive and pull back. Hell, Covid took me out for months and months, so I know the dance of having to cancel things and reprioritize your schedule because your energy just isn't there.

After my recent surgery, I obviously had to rest. That meant every non-essential or non-client task was taken off my calendar. I gave up marketing and speaking and did the bare minimum to keep my business going. There was a part of me that absolutely surrendered to that. I found some delightful shows on Netflix and really enjoyed binge-watching Ted Lasso.

I became used to this new level of energy and output. Sleeping as late as I needed to, having a few extra cookies, luxuriating with my beloved TV shows... but not walking the dog!

Coming from a person who has been used to striving and achieving her whole life, trust me... This was big. Truth is, though, I was restless. While I was allowing my body to stop and get the rest it needed, the part in me that is a driven, a high-achieving alpha woman was screaming. "I love marketing. I love creating. I love being more visible and being of higher service". Now I was conflicted. I had no energy to do anything but what I was doing, yet I was not at peace.

And here's what I learned. I made the huge discovery that my identity was tied to productivity. Let me say that again. I determined that if I wasn't a person who was working hard or had a thriving business, I would probably be boring, do nothing, and basically sit around watching bad reality shows eating gluten-free cookies.

The part that is always trying to protect us by making sure we do things and be who we've always been was going crazy because I was no longer willing to be who I had been.

This is what I have discovered, and I think it is a super important lesson if you relate to being a high-achieving/driven woman:

What if, to become untamed, uncensored, and unleashed, you had to stop?

What if, instead of going and doing and getting, you had to focus on receiving even more? What If instead of running high drive / masculine energy, you tapped into the feminine energy which is guided by intuition?

The truth is that the purest version of who you are can only be discovered with quiet reflection. But sadly, most women have bought into the myth that we are who we help. We are what we create. And if you are an alpha / driven woman, you might have the identity that is tied to your output and your income.

I want to invite you to let all that fall away. Now that might be scary. You might not know how or be convinced that you will be just a lazy slug eating bon-bons all day. But seriously, this is where we start.

When you strip all the "doing" and "striving" away, who are you at your core? Take your accomplishments and roles out of the mix, and what do you have left?

I'd encourage you to ask yourself this:

- Who am I?
- Who am I that is unchangeable?
- Who am I that has always been?
- Who is it that my soul shows up as?

These are powerful questions to meditate on. By doing this internal inventory using these questions, I came to know that who I am is love. The embodiment of love. It doesn't matter how much money I made or how many clients I serve or don't serve. I show up powerfully as love in all parts of my life.

This exercise was the beginning of unleashing me from the shackles of the false identity that I had before. So that's where I want you to start.

Who are YOU at your core? Taking away the roles and titles and successes and failures and history and things you are striving for or working toward, who are you? The goal here is to discover what part of you is true, what might be a persona, or an unconscious part that is rigid and interfering, and what is old "scar tissue" that can now be released.

Now, let me just say this: living in me is still very much an alpha woman. Living in me is a powerful creator that loves to reach out and have loads of meaningful connections and who has a huge soul mission.

Just because I got stopped and could no longer work in the way I was working; the yummy juicy life mission is still in there. I'm sharing this part because I don't want you to be afraid if you start to dismantle the false self or the personas that are keeping you on the hamster wheel.

You won't lose anything! It's only in stopping and evaluating that you will truly find peace.

The next place I would have you ponder is the question of, "What do you want to say?" Really. If you didn't have to worry about being politically correct, or if you weren't concerned about ruffling feathers or stepping on toes, or perhaps even appearing too big for your britches.... What would you like to say?

I take my clients on a guided visualization whereby I have them imagine that they are standing on a stage, filled with their God-given mission/purpose. They are so aware that this is theirs and theirs alone, and it is in Divine Right order that they live that and see it out to its highest expression.

Then they notice that their perfect clients are coming into the room. Clients who, on a soul level, have been chosen. Clients that would be the perfect fit to receive what they have. Now I have them stand there and speak their message. Speaking from the heart what they desire and what they know to be true. It's a super powerful exercise and I would encourage you to try that.

Sadly, women have been censored for centuries. I believe it is only in stopping, getting still, and receiving the message that we will understand how to speak our truth with power.

So be in the question. What do I want to say? Who do I want to say it to, and why does my message matter so much? If you keep asking, and give yourself permission to know, you will be given the answer!

My guidance to you is to no longer be afraid of saying no or stopping when you need to. Allow your wisdom to emerge from the inside. If you can look at your identity and begin to trust that what is happening is happening because it's supposed to and begin to trust what you are guided to do, even if it doesn't seem like the old you would do it, you are on the right path.

Wrapping up the story of my crazy hand injury, let me share where I am today.

Even though initially I was devastated and had to get loads and loads of healing support to get through the scary surgery journey, today I call it a blessing. It truly was one of those "it's not happening TO you, it's happening FOR you" events.

My fingers are still stiff, but my identity is flexible! My faith has deepened tremendously because I really, really leaned into trust when I was guided to "let it all go."

I feel so powerful as today I'm mightily connected to the TRUTH of my being and not the old "programmed" ways of showing up in the world that I had bought into.

So, let's make a deal, ok? Get some of these lessons without having to face injury and surgery and lots of pain!!!

One thing I always share with my clients is that-"the only way around is through." My wish for you is that you have the courage to look inside. Release what no longer serves you. Let go of others' ideas of success. Then tap into the truest part of you and build your life and business around that.

As women, we have so much power. By working with the divine feminine and learning to trust yourself, you will find a way to be, unleashed, untamed, and uncensored.

Peace and blessings!

ABOUT THE AUTHOR

Therese Skelly, M.A is the author of the best-selling book, *Love-Based Mission: How to Create a Business That Serves Your Soul.* She also hosts the highly inspirational Fiercely Brilliant podcast and is an in-demand guest on podcasts, live events, and summits.

Working with high achieving alpha females who have a huge mission in the world but no longer want to hustle and burn themselves out, Therese blends her twenty-five-year psychotherapist background with business coaching, marketing, and sales training, plus her signature "kick-ass" mama bear wisdom and love. She's a native of sunny Arizona and has the sun damage to prove it. She's also the proud mom to two amazing young men and one crazy cattle dog.

Website: www.ThereseSkelly.com
Facebook: www.facebook.com/therese.skelly
and www.facebook.com/groups/FierceWomeninBusiness
Podcast: www.thereseskelly.com/category/fiercely-brilliant-
    podcast
Instagram: www.instagram.com/thereseskelly

20

ABOUT AMA PUBLISHING

& ADRIANA MONIQUE ALVAREZ

"Writing a book is sacred. It's not easy, nor is it difficult. It is a holy act."
~Adriana Monique Alvarez

Being a life path number 3 means I have deep reverence for a clear vision, imagination and the joy of living. Creativity and self expression are my right and left hand.

So it makes sense that my soul thrives when I am assisting others in communicating the stories that matter to them.

As entrepreneurs, there's an added layer — our stories literally call in the people who we are meant to work with.

I am the first woman in my family to put my knowledge, experience, and wisdom in books that can be passed down through generations.

I suspect you might be a first as well.

This is a sacred calling.

It's been said that 85% of the population have the desire to write a book, but only 1% actually write and publish it.

The Mayans were a Mesoamerican civilization, noted for Maya script, the only known fully developed writing system of the pre-Columbian Americas, as well as for its art, architecture, mathematical and astronomical systems.

Their writing system was made up of 800 glyphs. Some of the glyphs were pictures and others represented sounds. They chiseled the glyphs into stone and inside codices.

Codices were books that were folded like an accordion. The pages were fig bark covered in white lime and bound in jaguar skins. The Mayans wrote hundreds of these books. They contained information on history, medicine, astronomy, and their religion. The Spanish missionaries burned all but four of these books.

The Ancient Mayans were a very religious people. Mayan actions were based on rituals and ceremonies.

I have been asked to return to the rituals and ceremonies that activate and invoke the writer within those who are being asked to write and release their stories in the world right now.

The first step is leaving the distractions that keep us busy, occupied, and convinced we don't have the resources — be it time, money, or energy — to write a book.

The second step is to connect to ourselves, the book that is calling us, and those who will read it.

The third step is action that is surrounded by support.

You don't need to know how to write and publish your book.

You don't need to know how to market your book.

You don't need to know how to make money from your book.

You simply must know YOU MUST DO IT.

You must know this is not a "someday" thing.

It's a "right now, sense of urgency, surrendering to the call" thing.

. . .

In December of 2016 I published my first book, *"Success Re-defined: Travel, Motherhood and Being the Boss."*

That book is what launched my online business. I had been offline before that and it allowed me to get 35 wonderful clients, right off the bat. It then led to me getting featured in publications like Forbes, International Living, and The Huffington Post, and I then went on to run a program just six months later that had over 100 clients in it.

Right after that I really felt this strong urge to help women write their own book and figure out how to get featured in publications just like I had done, so I ran a program called "Instant Authority" and it was magical… it was all clicking and coming together and I had plans of running and transitioning my business to where the focus would be on books and helping women communicate in a really powerful way.

However, just a few months later I found out there were major complications with my third pregnancy and I would later go on to lose that baby.

From that point on, all I have done is put one foot in front of the other. I've done my best to show up every single day to live this life in her honor, remembering to really be present with the two children that I do have with me, to having a wonderful relationship with my husband, and to pouring my heart into my clients and my business.

It was in April, 2019 that I felt like it was time to take the stream that had went dormant and bring it back, and it was an interesting thing because I had hired a new coach at that time, and she said, "I think you should move in the direction of books, and that you should make this part of your business model."

I ran with her idea because it was the confirmation that I needed, and since that time I have sold over 50 spots in these book collaborations.

This has been an amazing journey and what I want you to know is that this is what happens when you keep following your heart and keep putting one foot in front of the other.

There are times when entrepreneurship and business and dreams in life can be all over the place, but the key is is that we stay on the path.

Sometimes I think, "Why was this two-year detour part of my journey? What was that all about?"

And what I hear is that the people who were meant to be in the books with me, they weren't in my life yet, and I was not yet the woman who was going to lead them through those difficult times.

I was forced to dig deep, I was forced to find my most authentic voice, and now it's that much sweeter.

Since I've been announcing the books, I've had a lot of men approach me who want to be in books as well.

When I was doing business consulting I was really honoring the unique differences between men and women and how I could help women through both motherhood and business and navigating that and now I'm so excited to be opening the books up to have male contributors as well.

Adriana Monique Alvarez (AMA) Publishing would love to help you tell your story too. We have helped to publish authors through our course, through our multi-author books, and as solo authors.

Here's the thing... **Your story, it's ready to be told**.

Website: *www.AdrianaMoniqueAlvarez.com*
Facebook: *www.facebook.com/AdrianaMoniqueAlvarez*
Youtube: *www.youtube.com/c/AdrianaMoniqueAlvarez*

Printed in Great Britain
by Amazon

75779224R00115